Apress Pocket Guides

Apress Pocket Guides present concise summaries of cutting-edge developments and working practices throughout the tech industry. Shorter in length, books in this series aims to deliver quick-to-read guides that are easy to absorb, perfect for the time-poor professional.

This series covers the full spectrum of topics relevant to the modern industry, from security, AI, machine learning, cloud computing, web development, product design, to programming techniques and business topics too.

Typical topics might include:

- A concise guide to a particular topic, method, function or framework

- Professional best practices and industry trends

- A snapshot of a hot or emerging topic

- Industry case studies

- Concise presentations of core concepts suited for students and those interested in entering the tech industry

- Short reference guides outlining 'need-to-know' concepts and practices.

More information about this series at https://link.springer.com/bookseries/17385.

Cybersecurity for Everyone

A Human-Centered Approach to Protecting Yourself and Your Community

Cathy Olieslaeger

Apress®

Cybersecurity for Everyone: A Human-Centered Approach to Protecting Yourself and Your Community

Cathy Olieslaeger
Durham, NC, USA

ISBN-13 (pbk): 979-8-8688-1407-5   ISBN-13 (electronic): 979-8-8688-1408-2
https://doi.org/10.1007/979-8-8688-1408-2

Managing Director, Apress Media LLC: Welmoed Spahr
Acquisitions Editor: Susan McDermott
Development Editor: Laura Berendson
Project Manager: Jessica Vakili

Distributed to the book trade worldwide by Springer Science+Business Media New York, 1 New York Plaza, New York, NY 10004. Phone 1-800-SPRINGER, fax (201) 348-4505, e-mail orders-ny@springer-sbm.com, or visit www.springeronline.com. Apress Media, LLC is a California LLC and the sole member (owner) is Springer Science + Business Media Finance Inc (SSBM Finance Inc). SSBM Finance Inc is a **Delaware** corporation.

For information on translations, please e-mail booktranslations@springernature.com; for reprint, paperback, or audio rights, please e-mail bookpermissions@springernature.com.

Apress titles may be purchased in bulk for academic, corporate, or promotional use. eBook versions and licenses are also available for most titles. For more information, reference our Print and eBook Bulk Sales web page at https://www.apress.com/gp/services/source-code.

If disposing of this product, please recycle the paper

Table of Contents

About the Author

Cathy Olieslaeger founded The Triangle Net LLC with the vision of a world where cybersecurity is embedded in society's educational and organizational practices, where social equality and meritocracy are the norm, and where all misfits are given an opportunity to reach their full potential.

The mission of The Triangle Net is to make a large-scale and immediate impact on the cybersecurity talent gap through collaboration, structural change, social engagement, and early education. The Triangle Net connects people with opportunities to learn, work, and support others in cybersecurity.

To raise awareness of the endless opportunities in cybersecurity, Cathy started a podcast called *Journey into Cybersecurity*. This podcast provides a diverse cast of role models, so young people can see them in their shoes. You can't be what you can't see.

Before becoming an independent Cybersecurity Advisor, Cathy was employed by CyberSaint Security as their Customer Success Director, supporting organizations and cybersecurity consulting firms to strengthen and mature their cybersecurity risk management program. She also worked for Agio Inc., Verizon Business, Orange Business Services, and Belgacom North America.

Cathy enjoys volunteering and is a founding board member of Tweens & Technology, a NC-based nonprofit dedicated to early STEM, including cybersecurity, education.

ABOUT THE AUTHOR

Cathy is an eternal student of everything cyber and leadership. She completed her Executive MBA with the Jack Welch Management Institute, as well as ISACA's CISM, (ISC)2's CISSP, and CMMC Certified Professional certifications in recent years to grow into an executive cybersecurity advisory role.

Cathy lives by the motto taught by Brendon Burchard: Live, Love, Matter.

About the Technical Reviewer

Jacqui Pomales is an advocate for empowering kids with the tools and knowledge they need to navigate the ever-evolving world of technology. With 20+ years of leadership experience in corporate marketing, event management, and operations, Jacqui has honed a unique blend of technical expertise and practical advice, making complex tech concepts accessible to all. Jacqui partners with business and community leaders and technology organizations to get them engaged and help educate children to confidently explore the tech-driven world while staying secure.

With a focus on building a safer, more inclusive tech landscape, Jacqui continues to be a trusted voice in the conversation about how to responsibly support families and the community in a tech-driven world.

Acknowledgments

I wouldn't be who I am today without my two sons. As a single mother of two cute and energetic little toddlers, working in the NY Metro area and running the rat race every day at the cusp of the financial crisis of 2008, failure was not an option. Everything I ever did was for them. I wasn't the best at anything, but I would give my darndest best to be a good mother to them, a rock they could always stand on, a place they could call home so they could be themselves, feel safe, and thrive. Nothing gives me greater joy and a sense of gratitude than the privilege of calling Nico and Leo my sons.

It is the "never quit" and a growth mindset combo that led me to a job at Verizon Business where I discovered the massive domain of cybersecurity. Anne Smith and Jim Stupak hired me for a job I had never done before, a stretch by any stretch of the imagination. They saw something in me I didn't even see. My experience at Verizon as a regional strategic sales overlay followed by a business transformation program management role changed my trajectory permanently. It is there where I found my purpose to join the cybersecurity community. I wanted to be part of the solution, not the problem. I needed to know and keep learning so I could better protect my family from harm.

My colleagues at Verizon Business were all driven, collaborative, willing to learn, and welcoming. While I worked with more amazing people than I can count on all fingers and toes, I owe a great amount of gratitude to Howard Belger, Mike Ruhnke, Steven Springer, Don Mercier, Ron Zajac, Matt Brodtman, Mireille Bueti, Eleanor Diodatti, Tara Barros, Jodie Hitchman, and Lisa Gonsales for their leadership, inspiration, support, and collaboration. The lessons learned and experiences shared will always stay with me.

ACKNOWLEDGMENTS

Thanks to my boys, I had the opportunity to volunteer within the PTA of their middle and high schools. I learned how underfunded schools and teachers are and how important community support is in the education of our children. During career day, I recognized how few children knew the concept or purpose of cybersecurity. That is how Robert Martin from the Raleigh ISSA chapter and Derrick Thompson from Tweens & Technology entered my humble existence and showed me a path of community service. They brought STEM and cybersecurity education to the children in our local schools and community and welcomed me in their circle of amazing people.

As I gained a stronger footing in the cybersecurity domain, I was given the opportunity to work for Agio thanks to Laurie Leigh, Chris Harper, Garvin McKee, and Bart McDonough. I learned so much about cybersecurity programs, technical testing, and security operations again thanks to their willingness to see beyond my shortcomings and teach me how to be successful. I wouldn't be where I am today without the mentorship and friendship of Laurie Leigh, Gina Yacone, and Natalie Jreisat who remain my cheerleaders to this day.

For similar reasons, I am grateful that Steve Torino and Mike Glaser gave me the opportunity to join CyberSaint Security where I expanded my knowledge of GRC and learned so much about the cutting edge of cyber risk management using risk quantification and automation. This is also where I was given my first real leadership role where I was responsible for a team of customer success managers. My collaboration with Stephen Bueno, Keaton Fisher, Mary Rush, Ty Everton, Hayley Pruett, Jeff Wilson, James Simpson III, and many more has taught me so much and pushed me beyond what I thought myself capable of.

I found inspiration in the many people I've met through the Raleigh ISSA cybersecurity community, but especially in the people who were willing to participate in my little podcast, *Journey into Cybersecurity*. Many of them didn't know me, but they saw the importance of sharing their story to help young people and aspiring cybersecurity professionals to see themselves in their shoes. These podcast guests lit a fire in me and ignited the idea of writing a book about people in cybersecurity. Thank you, Gina Yacone, Jon Sternstein, Frances Baldwin, Derrick Thompson, Robert Martin, Gaylynn Fassler, Nia Lucky, Mark Fitzner, Alan Nobles, De'Von Carter, Antonio Chousa, Kelsey Cueto, Stefan Laneman, Anthony Picarello, Sarah Pinson, Jamila Blackwell, Adrianne George, Nathan Hicks, and Collin Roach. And while Emily Ellis's interview never made it to the published list, her story and friendship are part of this beautiful quilt of inspirational souls. They share the same purpose to protect their community, to help others on their journey, and to lead by example. My dream is that one day people will reach out to them and tell them how their story inspired them to also pursue a career in cybersecurity, to believe and invest in themselves so they too can reach the mountain top and live a purposeful life.

I would not have written this book if it weren't for my friend and community leader, Jacqui Pomales. Jacqui was introduced to me when I joined the board of Tweens & Technology. My world has changed ever since for the better. Jacqui embodies the term "selfless leader." Her grace, kindness, and unrivaled dedication to her community gave me the inspiration and determination to invest in my community through Tweens & Technology and to write this book. I am so honored she devoted her time and energy to the technical review of this book. I'm not sure how I will ever be able to repay her.

Finally, I want to thank my parents, Alice and Willy; my sister, Christine; my nephews, Mathias and Dorian; and my BFFs, Christel and Katia, for giving me the strength and encouragement to keep going and pursuing all my crazy dreams far away from our little town, Hoeilaart, in Belgium. I may have lived in the United States for the majority of my life, but you will always be my home.

CHAPTER 1

Start with Why

Why Start with Why and Not What

What gets you up in the morning? What moves you forward? What do you believe? What is your purpose? Do you ever pause and wonder why you do what you do?

Simon Sinek challenged our way of thinking, marketing, and leading in his *Golden Circle* TED Talk and *Start with Why* book. He shares how leaders like Martin Luther King Jr. and organizations like Apple inspired millions of people to believe in their dream and vision for a greater future for humanity and the imperative of challenging the status quo. It wasn't about the how or the what. It was about their vision, their why, first and foremost.

In cybersecurity, we are making the mistake of talking about the what and the how. We're not starting with why any of it matters. We're not starting with our shared purpose. We fail to inspire as we fail in our communication.

So let's get this book off on a good start. Let's start with why you matter and why cybersecurity should matter to you.

Your time is limited. Don't waste it living someone else's life.

—Steve Jobs

© Cathy Olieslaeger 2025
C. Olieslaeger, *Cybersecurity for Everyone*, Apress Pocket Guides,
https://doi.org/10.1007/979-8-8688-1408-2_1

Why for Children

Why do children as young as 5 want to be a doctor? Why does an 18-year-old embark on a very long medical learning journey? Is it because they like being around blood, trauma, disease, or worse? Do 12-hour shifts on their feet sound appealing? Does medical school seem easy?

Why do children as young as 5 want to be a firefighter or a police officer? Does it look easy? Do they like danger?

At a very early age, children see themselves performing heroic acts of selflessness. They want to help others. They want to give the gift of caring. They want to serve the greater good. They want and need to matter. That's it. They matter.

To compel a child, student, or adult to pursue anything, it must meet their natural need for a purpose. They need to belong to something bigger than themselves.

How do we represent cybersecurity in school or professionally? Do we make it about saving people, protecting our family and those we love, serving the greater good? No. And that's exactly why we have a lack of students and professionals pursuing a cybersecurity career. That is why the bad guys are winning, and we are losing trillions of dollars in economic value that could have been invested in our children and their future. We mess up the why. Royally.

Cybersecurity is not part of the K-12 educational curriculum (yet). The topic remains unknown or misunderstood. The only exception at the time of writing this book is North Dakota. In 2023, North Dakota became the first state in the United States making cybersecurity a mandatory subject in K-12.

In addition, cybersecurity is portrayed and only taught as a technical subject matter. Coding seems to be a mandatory element of the cybersecurity learning path, and, let's admit it, not many kids or adults are seeing any fun in coding. Yet, cybersecurity is so much more than that. It's actually not about coding at all, if I dare to say. Let's unpack that in the following chapters...

To make cybersecurity a subject worth pursuing, investing countless hours of education and work in, and overcoming endless challenges, we need to *start with why*. Cybersecurity is a field where anyone can make a positive impact using their unique skills, strengths, experiences, and perspectives. It is a domain with lots of opportunities to thrive and succeed no matter where you come from. People who work in cybersecurity perform heroic acts every single day: they keep the bad guys out and protect the good ones. Let us make that message more central to our educational and professional recruitment practices. *You matter*. We all matter. And it matters that we all invest in cybersecurity whether in our personal or professional lives.

The future of our children is in the balance. Their future is being decided right now.

Never say you can't do it. Say I haven't done it yet.

—Rick Rubin

Why for You and the Rest of Us

Think cybersecurity doesn't apply to you? Think again. The truth of the matter is that cybersecurity is something that should be important to everyone, no matter how old you are, what you do, where you live, and so forth. Cybersecurity has many connotations. People make assumptions about the topic, and they may dismiss it as something that doesn't matter to them. Parents, teachers, students, employers, and business leaders to some degree don't want to deal with it. It's not something they want to worry about; they're too busy with more important things. There's a knowledge gap around cybersecurity that stems from the exponential growth in technology and our inability to keep up with it all. We cannot blame anyone.

Cybercrime has permeated the technological fabric of our world, and it is ruining lives everywhere. Nobody is immune from this threat. Whether it's sextortion leading children to commit suicide, human trafficking, pig butchering leading to financial ruin, or ransomware attacks closing down hospitals leading to patients dying, someone is making money off of the pain and harm they cause to people. But there is more! Disinformation campaigns on social media, radicalizing people into weapons for hire, or the intrusion of the utilities we depend on such as electricity and water are growing in scale. People are being manipulated, blindsided, and robbed left and right. Organizations are losing their ability to innovate and grow. If our cyber defenses are not getting better, cybercrime and its short- and long-term aftermath will only get worse.

Every person is either the weakest link or the strongest defense to their own personal life or the organization they study, work, or volunteer at. Understanding that you play a part in protecting your life and those around you is the most important message I want to share with you. It is not as hard or complicated as you may think. You need a few tricks in your tool bag. Let's hook you up!

Courage is not the absence of fear, but the triumph over it.

—Nelson Mandela

Why for Me

This book's why is simple: to bring cybersecurity into your home, your school, and as soon as you set foot at work. This book's goal is to make cybersecurity embedded in our habits, systems, and society. This is a stab at providing an affordable, accessible solution that makes it easy to understand why it matters that you protect yourself and those you love and how to do just that. This is also an effort to make cybersecurity a potential career path for more people of all backgrounds, addressing a talent and – very importantly – a diversity gap that permeates the STEM field. I truly hope this helps you on your journey as we are all in this together.

The ultimate goal is to reverse the downward spiral we're on, losing billions of economic value that could go to our children's education (imagine a world where education is affordable), the safety and democracy we all depend on (imagine a world where the truth is all you see on social media or news outlets), and a future where everyone can thrive (imagine a world where we don't compete against each other, but collaborate to solve real-world problems).

Simon Sinek shares in his interview with Steve Bartlett on the *Diary of a CEO* podcast that the ultimate and truest purpose is to serve those who serve others. This book and everything I do is in pursuit of my ultimate purpose: to serve you in protecting you and yours.

Let's go!

The people who are crazy enough to think they can change the world are the ones who do.

—Steve Jobs

CHAPTER 2

Journey into Cybersecurity

The Genesis

The 2020 COVID-19 pandemic was a tumultuous and challenging time. The air was filled with uncertainty and fear. We all were faced with our own mortality and the terrifying possibility of losing a loved one. We were grasping for ideas to get through those days without losing our lives or our minds. I wanted to do something that mattered and made my finite time on this precious earth worthwhile. I decided to create a podcast that would put a spotlight on the endless opportunities in cybersecurity. I wanted to provide diverse role models to young people who were still weighing their educational options.

You can't be what you can't see.

—Marian Wright Edelman

Cybersecurity needs to grow in diversity from a demographic perspective and beyond. I wanted to change that by sharing inspirational stories of women and men of all walks of life who also happen to work in cybersecurity. I wanted to give cybersecurity a new face and break away

© Cathy Olieslaeger 2025
C. Olieslaeger, *Cybersecurity for Everyone*, Apress Pocket Guides,
https://doi.org/10.1007/979-8-8688-1408-2_2

from the white male in a hoodie stereotype. *Journey into Cybersecurity* was born in the Fall of 2020, and I cannot tell you what an uplifting experience it has been to learn and share the unique stories of these wonderful people.

When time became a very finite and precious thing and human connection became constrained, I found hope and inspiration one podcast interview at a time. I would like to share the lessons learned, common threads, and important takeaways from this endeavor and my own journey into cybersecurity. I hope this will inspire you to take action, join the Cyber Hero Squad and share my hope and optimism for a better future.

Pushing Boundaries and Sharing the Love

On the podcast, I always ask my guests what they were like as a kid and what they wanted to be growing up. It is no surprise to anyone when I say none of them dreamed of being a cybersecurity professional. From scientist, athlete, writer to astronaut, they all had different aspirations. Yet, here they are, playing a part in protecting the rest of us in cyber.

I was my parents' last hope of having a boy. I had a cute short haircut until about age 10 and was raised to help out with any and all chores in the house, the garage or yard. We lived in a small town in Belgium where everyone either knew or was related to the other. Most people in my immediate circle worked locally in a small business. The types of role models and my worldview were a bit limited. It was nice growing up in a bubble to be honest. To me as a child, the world was a safe place.

Because expectations of me (and most girls in those days) were pretty low, I didn't quite know what to expect of myself either. Other than being a multilingual wannabe Broadway dancer, I had no vision for my future. I just felt there was more to discover. Eventually, I did venture out and have been pushing the boundaries, all of them, ever since. That drive led me to study abroad and eventually move to the United States, where I unexpectedly landed my first job in telecom – and from there, the journey truly began. Each step in my career brought new challenges and learning opportunities. But it wasn't until I began to understand the growing cyber threats while at Verizon Business that I found my true calling. I knew I had to step up, to shift from being a bystander to becoming part of the solution in cybersecurity.

The creation of The Triangle Net, an initiative to support the cybersecurity community and help people find opportunities to learn, work, and support each other has been my first brainchild, along with the *Journey into Cybersecurity* podcast, which then led to public speaking engagements at cybersecurity conferences and local schools. This book is meant to collect all the lessons learned with my personal spin on it, a challenge to look at this picture in different ways. I am challenging you to challenge the status quo with me. There is so much power and potential in collaboration, sharing knowledge and unique perspectives. Let's learn, work, and grow together, and venture on a journey into cybersecurity one step at a time.

> *If you're not getting outside of your comfort zone, then you're not growing.*
>
> —Chad Foster

CHAPTER 3

Common Misconceptions

Cybersecurity Is Not My Problem

I learned about the *fixed mindset* in the book by Dr. Carol S. Dweck called *Mindset*. She explains that people with a fixed mindset see the world and themselves in black or white. They eventually avoid learning and being coined a failure. This is a result of an environment where the fixed mindset dominates. Our schools are very good at turning kids who make mistakes and fail tests into adults who fear failure so much they don't even bother trying.

© Cathy Olieslaeger 2025
C. Olieslaeger, *Cybersecurity for Everyone*, Apress Pocket Guides,
https://doi.org/10.1007/979-8-8688-1408-2_3

Could this be why some people shy away from learning about cybersecurity? They brush it off, convincing themselves it's not their concern, it's too technical or they won't be affected by this cybercrime stuff. And with that, they dismiss it entirely.

The growth mindset on the other hand embraces learning, being challenged, trying new strategies, and finding fulfillment in the process and not in a test result, a grade, a job title, or other defining labels.

What if the fear of failure is stopping us from protecting ourselves against cyber threats?

People with a fixed mindset are easy targets to cybercriminals. They don't care to learn about the threats, changing technology, and how to protect themselves. But bad actors don't care. They love collecting your personal information, your credit card number, your work credentials that you also use for your social media accounts, and so on and so forth. Whether you are aware or not, you are part of the attack surface as long as you are connected to the Internet.

To be part of the solution, you need to recognize that you too play an instrumental role in learning and sharing cybersecurity knowledge. If we all open our minds and see the cyber threat as a real threat to any of us, then we can come together and create better solutions and actually win this battle. Imagine all the millions and billions of dollars organizations and governments can invest in education, safety, infrastructure, innovation, collaboration, and better wages. Isn't that worth your time and energy?

Cybersecurity Is Rocket Science

Cybersecurity is a big domain. Compare it to the medical field. Not everyone is a brain surgeon. There are many people who support the delivery of healthcare to others, and most don't perform brain surgery.

Look at cybersecurity as an end goal and shared objective, like the medical field's goal is good health. We can all contribute to making our society safer than it is today. Everyone's unique skills, strengths, and perspectives are key in making our society safer. Once you recognize this as a fact of life, nothing can really get in your way of joining the Cyber Hero Squad. You don't need to be a rocket scientist after all! Together, we make a real difference.

Cybersecurity Is (Too) Technical

Absolutely not! Look at cybersecurity as a way to be safe in a technologically driven world. You wear a seatbelt in your car; use a good endpoint protection solution on your smartphone or computer. You wear a helmet when you bike; use a two-factor authenticator to protect your personal data that you store in the cloud. You get your car serviced on a regular basis; update your devices on a regular basis. It's the small stuff that starts to add up if you do it consistently and regularly. So don't let technology slow you down; embrace it and use it to your own advantage, your safety.

When it comes to pursuing a career in cybersecurity, there are alternative learning paths to the technical ones that you see most widely adopted. I will cover those in depth in future chapters.

Cybersecurity Is Only for Geeks

Everyone is using technology. Either that makes us all geeks or it means we all need to know how to use technology securely. Your safety and that of your loved ones depend on it. You learned how to talk, walk, swim, drive a car, operate a smartphone, and use all kinds of applications that are transforming lives. Learning cybersecurity is just one additional step in your growth and development. Go ahead, unleash your inner geek. You got this!

Cybersecurity Is Not a Business Function

Many adults did not learn about computers or any kind of technology in school. Some of them are running organizations and may not have kept up with the fast-paced change in technology and the cyber threats. To them, cybersecurity sounds like an IT thing; it sounds technical. It wasn't part of their MBA program; therefore, it is not a business function.

Leadership must understand the significant impact of cyber threats and take proactive steps to establish cybersecurity best practices. CEOs can no longer ignore the reality of cybercrime or cyber warfare; these threats will inevitably affect their business. In addition, negligence and inaction can be found a criminal act. CEOs and their leadership team now bear the responsibility to manage cyber risk from the top down. If they don't and they operate in the financial services, healthcare, critical infrastructure, consumer services, or part of the supply chain to governments or they are publicly traded, they will have a serious reckoning with regulators and business stakeholders wherever they may be doing business.

The threat to the supply chains that we all depend on is real and mounting. Cybercrime or insecurity is considered one of the top five existential threats to organizations and society. Cyberattacks are on the same list of risks as extreme weather caused by global warming, AI-generated misinformation and disinformation, social and/or political polarization, and the cost of living crisis. If your utilities, food, and water supplies can be disrupted, then your life can be affected in very dramatic ways. This is why organizations no matter how small and their leadership are being held accountable to a higher standard when it comes to managing cyber security risk. We are all in this together!

As more and more organizations are faced with cybercrime and serious financial losses, the cost thereof is offset by increasing the prices of their products and services. That's right. If you want inflation to stop messing up your personal or business's bottom line, we need to fight cybercrime head-on, all of us.

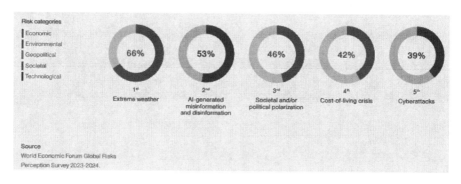

Risk categories
| Economic
| Environmental
| Geopolitical
| Societal
| Technological

66% — 1st — Extreme weather

53% — 2nd — AI-generated misinformation and disinformation

46% — 3rd — Societal and/or political polarization

42% — 4th — Cost-of-living crisis

39% — 5th — Cyberattacks

Source
World Economic Forum Global Risks
Perception Survey 2023-2024.

CHAPTER 4

We're Losing

The Status Quo Is Not Looking Good

Each year, reports are published on the cyber threats, incidents, and breaches that resulted from them. They have different data sources or vantage points, so it's always a good idea to review more than one. Here are a few worth subscribing to:

- FBI Internet Crime Report: IC3 Annual Report

- Crowdstrike Global Threat Report

- Google: Mandiant's M-Trends Report

- The Verizon Data Breach Investigations Report (DBIR)

- Palo Alto Unit 42 Incident Response Report

- IBM Cost of a Data Breach Report

The common trend in all these reports every single year is that the bad news is getting worse and the bad guys are winning more and more. More individuals, families, and organizations of all shapes and sizes are being attacked, and they are suffering bigger financial losses. Cybercrime is big business.

© Cathy Olieslaeger 2025
C. Olieslaeger, *Cybersecurity for Everyone*, Apress Pocket Guides,
https://doi.org/10.1007/979-8-8688-1408-2_4

What's the difference between an incident and a breach?

- **Incident**: A cybersecurity event that may have a negative impact on the organization affected. For example, someone clicked a malicious link in their email.

- **Breach**: An incident that resulted in the loss of data. For example, after someone clicked a malicious link, malware was deployed on that user's computer, and the malicious actor was able to exfiltrate data from it.

IC3: FBI Internet Crime Report for 2023

In the United States, everyone can report a cybercrime they are affected by with the Internet Crime Complaint Center (IC3). This information is tallied up in an annual report in collaboration with the FBI and shows how individuals are targeted and how the attacks vary depending on the demographic of the victims. The biggest lesson from this report is that no age group is safe from cybercrime.

2023 - COMPLAINANTS BY AGE GROUP [13]

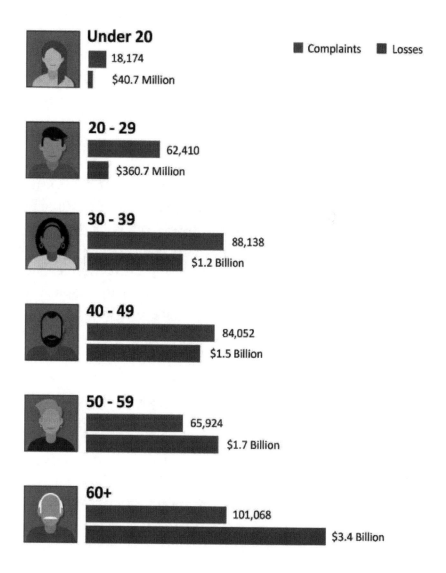

Under 20
18,174
$40.7 Million

■ Complaints   ■ Losses

20 - 29
62,410
$360.7 Million

30 - 39
88,138
$1.2 Billion

40 - 49
84,052
$1.5 Billion

50 - 59
65,924
$1.7 Billion

60+
101,068
$3.4 Billion

"In 2023, IC3 received a record number of complaints from the American public: 880,418 complaints were registered, with potential losses exceeding $12.5 billion. This is a nearly 10% increase in complaints received, and it represents a 22% increase in losses suffered, compared to 2022. As impressive as these figures appear, we know they are conservative regarding cybercrime in 2023. Consider that when the FBI recently infiltrated the Hive ransomware group's infrastructure, we found that only about 20% of Hive's victims reported to law enforcement."

"The past year, investment fraud was once again the costliest type of crime tracked by IC3. Losses to investment scams rose from $3.31 billion in 2022 to $4.57 billion in 2023—a 38% increase. The second-costliest type of crime was business e-mail compromise (BEC), with 21,489 complaints amounting to $2.9 billion in reported losses. Tech support scams, meanwhile, were the third-costliest type of crime tracked by IC3. Notably, different age groups tended to be impacted by different crimes. Victims 30 to 49 years old were the most likely group to report losses from investment fraud, while the elderly accounted for well over half of losses to tech support scams."

"In 2023, ransomware incidents continued to be impactful and costly. After a brief downturn in 2022, ransomware incidents were again on the rise with over 2,825 complaints. This represents an increase of 18% from 2022. Reported losses rose 74%, from $34.3 million to $59.6 million. Cybercriminals continue to adjust their tactics, and the FBI has observed emerging ransomware trends, such as the deployment of multiple ransomware variants against the same victim and the use of data-destruction tactics to increase pressure on victims to negotiate."

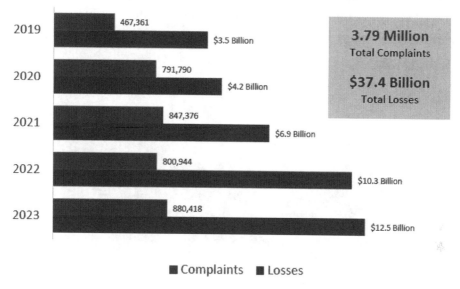

Complaints and Losses over the Last Five Years*

2019 — 467,361 — $3.5 Billion
2020 — 791,790 — $4.2 Billion
2021 — 847,376 — $6.9 Billion
2022 — 800,944 — $10.3 Billion
2023 — 880,418 — $12.5 Billion

3.79 Million
Total Complaints

$37.4 Billion
Total Losses

■ Complaints   ■ Losses

CrowdStrike 2024 Global Threat Report

"Today's cyber threats are particularly alarming due to the widespread use of hands-on or "interactive intrusion" techniques, which involve adversaries actively executing actions on a host to accomplish their objectives. Unlike malware attacks that depend on the deployment of malicious tooling and scripts, interactive intrusions leverage the creativity and problem-solving skills of human adversaries. These individuals can mimic expected user and administrator behavior, making it difficult for defenders to differentiate between legitimate user activity and a cyberattack."

"In 2023, CrowdStrike observed a 60% year-over-year increase in the number of interactive intrusion campaigns, with a 73% increase in the second half compared to 2022."

"Today's sophisticated cyberattacks only take minutes to succeed. Adversaries use techniques such as interactive hands-on-keyboard attacks and legitimate tools to attempt to hide from detection. To further accelerate attack tempo, adversaries can access credentials in multiple ways, including purchasing them from access brokers for a few hundred dollars. Organizations must prioritize protecting identities in 2024."

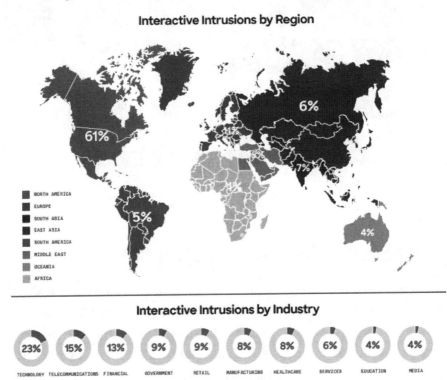

Interactive Intrusions by Region

Interactive Intrusions by Industry

TECHNOLOGY	TELECOMMUNICATIONS	FINANCIAL	GOVERNMENT	RETAIL	MANUFACTURING	HEALTHCARE	SERVICES	EDUCATION	MEDIA
23%	15%	13%	9%	9%	8%	8%	6%	4%	4%

Mandiant's M-Trends 2024

"Mandiant tracks more than 4,000 threat groups, 719 of which were newly tracked in 2023. Mandiant investigators encountered 316 different threat groups when responding to intrusions in 2023, 220 groups were both newly tracked and observed in Mandiant investigations in 2023. These counts are largely in line with 2022 observations. For example in 2022, 265 groups were both newly tracked and observed in Mandiant investigations. In 2023, organizations faced intrusions by two named advanced persistent threat

(APT) groups from Russia and Iran; four named financial threat (FIN) groups; and 310 uncategorized (UNC) groups. While 253 of these UNC groups were newly identified, Mandiant has tracked the remaining 57 UNC groups for periods ranging from one to 10 years. This distribution of threat groups suggests that organizations contend with both established and new threats on a regular basis."

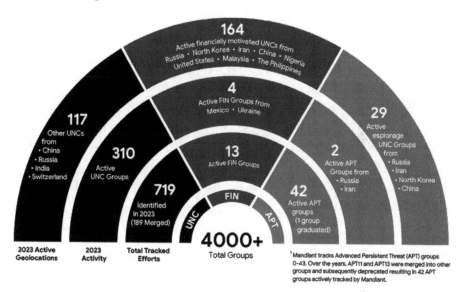

Verizon's 2024 Data Breach Investigations Report

"Roughly one-third of all breaches involved Ransomware or some other Extortion technique. Pure Extortion attacks have risen over the past year and are now a component of 9% of all breaches. The shift of traditional ransomware actors toward these newer techniques resulted in a bit of a decline in Ransomware to 23%. However, when combined, given that they share threat actors, they represent a strong growth to 32% of breaches. Ransomware was a top threat across 92% of industries."

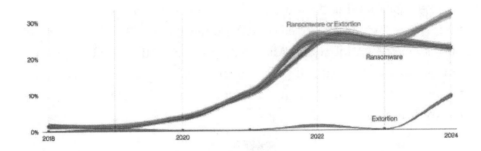

Palo Alto 2024 Unit 42 Incident Response Report

Initial access

"Attackers exploited software vulnerabilities to gain access 36% more often in 2023 than previous years... and that trend is continuing in 2024."

Data theft tactics

"In 93% of incidents Unit 42 responded to, threat actors took data indiscriminately rather than searching for specific data."

IBM Cost of a Data Breach Report 2024

Average total cost of a breach

"The average cost of a data breach jumped to USD 4.88 million from USD 4.45 million in 2023, a 10% spike and the highest increase since the pandemic. A rise in the cost of lost business, including operational downtime and lost customers, and the cost of post-breach responses, such as staffing customer service help desks and paying higher regulatory fines, drove this increase. Taken together, these costs totaled USD 2.8 million, the highest combined amount for lost business and post-breach activities over the past 6 years."

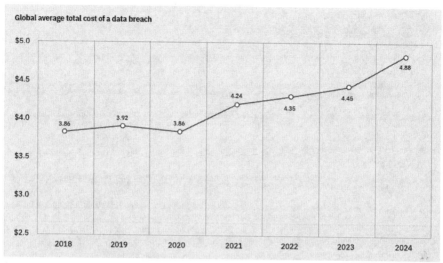

Figure 1. Measured in USD millions

Average cost of a malicious insider attack

"Compared to other vectors, malicious insider attacks resulted in the highest costs, averaging USD 4.99 million. Among other expensive attack vectors were business email compromise, phishing, social engineering, and stolen or compromised credentials. Gen AI may be playing a role in creating some of these phishing attacks. For example, gen AI makes it easier than ever for even non-English speakers to produce grammatically correct and plausible phishing messages."

Share of breaches involving customer personal data

"Nearly half of all breaches involved customer personal identifiable information (PII), which can include tax identification (ID) numbers, emails, phone numbers and home addresses. Intellectual property (IP) records came in a close second (43% of breaches). The cost of IP records jumped considerably from last year, to USD 173 per record in this year's study from USD 156 per record in last year's report."

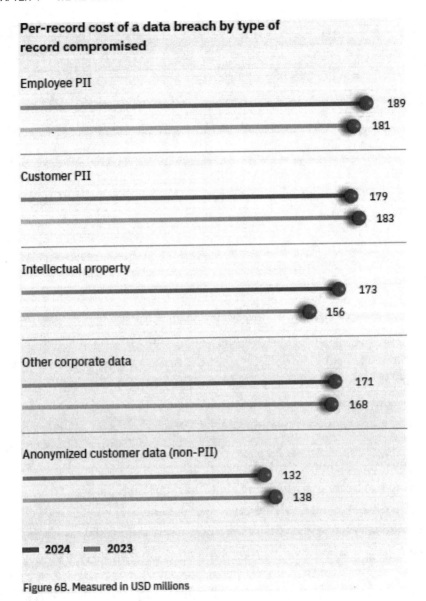

Per-record cost of a data breach by type of record compromised

Employee PII
- 189
- 181

Customer PII
- 179
- 183

Intellectual property
- 173
- 156

Other corporate data
- 171
- 168

Anonymized customer data (non-PII)
- 132
- 138

■ 2024 ■ 2023

Figure 6B. Measured in USD millions

Growth of the cyber skills shortage

"More than half of breached organizations are facing high levels of security staffing shortages. This issue represents a 26.2% increase from the prior year, a situation that corresponded to an average USD 1.76 million more in breach costs. Even as 1 in 5 organizations say they used some form of gen AI security tools—which are expected to help close the gap by boosting productivity and efficiency—this skills gap remains a challenge."

> *Insanity is doing the same thing over and over and expecting different results.*
>
> —Albert Einstein

Within the cybersecurity community, there is no lack of effort to keep up with the latest mouse traps. Technology keeps changing and so does the threat landscape. It's a constant whack-a-mole game. There are lots of associations and conferences that invest in the sharing of knowledge and best practices. Despite these efforts, the bad guys keep winning. The volume of cybercrime is growing, and the financial losses to individuals and organizations are only increasing. How come?

We keep doing the same things over and over again and are expecting different results. We are missing something, something big. If we don't change our approach and our mindset, cybercrime, and by extension cyberwar, may become an existential threat to more and more people. Even if you live under a rock, it can affect you too.

The question that keeps me up at night is: Why are we losing ground in cybersecurity despite our best efforts?

We must challenge the status quo. Let's challenge ourselves, our definition of the problem, and our idea of a solution. Let's think big!

Cybersecurity Is a Boys' Club

Much of the technology world is represented by men; cybersecurity isn't any different. Go ahead, roll your eyes, and ask what else is new?!

Could it be that our assumptions about who's responsible to solve the diversity gap (hopefully you agree that this is a problem) and how to solve it are flawed? Could we be mistaken to think this is not our problem to solve?

Let me share why this matters and why we must address the diversity gap in tech, and in cybersecurity more specifically, as soon as possible. 9/11, i.e., September 11, 2001, is a day we will always remember. The events of that day shook us to our core. It all seemed unimaginable, completely surreal. Yet in a split second, the horror and aftermath of the biggest terrorist attack in the United States became a reality. It was a massive shock to the system, to our way of life, and the way we felt ever since.

In the CIA, a group of analysts within the counterterrorism unit knew it was a matter of when, not if, Osama Bin Laden's Al Qaeda would strike the United States within its own borders. This unit called Alec Station was greatly undervalued, underfunded, and underresourced. In spite of this, they had been collecting intelligence for years on Osama Bin Laden and Al Qaeda. They wrote many reports, issued many warnings, and provided many recommendations to capture Osama Bin Laden for multiple years. Years!

Their voices had been dismissed, muted for the longest time. Once their reports and warnings made it to the higher levels of command, they were not met with the sense of urgency they warranted. Those analysts were women.

To be a woman and get in the CIA back in the 1990s, let alone earlier, was a feat in and of itself. From recruitment to training, job placement to promotion, the path was ridden with obstacles and lots of No Men. (Not sure if that's a word, but we all know what a Yes Man is.) Women in the CIA are brilliant, strong, dedicated, and hardworking. They had to be the best in their class to even be considered for a job in the CIA, a perfect boys' club.

When all the federal buildings in Washington, DC, were being evacuated on 9/11, the women of Alec Station stayed.

9/11 was called an intelligence failure. The analysts of Alec Station were called to Congress to explain how all this happened. Isn't it ironic how the people in charge of funding are always blaming those they've been underfunding to begin with? Could this be a fixed mindset? Could this be a leadership weakness? Do we have a blind spot at the top?

Let's be blunt. 9/11 was a communication failure. The intelligence was there, black on white, but those who received the message did not listen and act on it. When it came time to point fingers, it was very easy to blame the messengers, women. "Shame on them, those women!" This is why the election of governmental leadership is not something we should take lightly. They decide who gets funding and who doesn't. They are ultimately responsible for funding or underfunding national security and making cybersecurity a priority or not.

Guess what, cybersecurity in most organizations is underfunded, underresourced, and critically undervalued. Yet, it is *only a matter of when, not if,* a major cyber incident occurs. We cannot afford another "intelligence failure" because the next one will start in the virtual world and will affect our physical world without needing hijacked planes or shoe bombs. With the growing adoption of artificial intelligence (AI), botnets, and deep fakes by malicious actors and power-hungry nation states, the odds and risks are only increasing. The stakes are just too high to keep our heads stuck in the sand and keep our ways stuck in the 20th century.

In her TED Talk, Mary Ann Sieghart talks about an authority gap explaining that men are assumed competent unless they prove otherwise and women are assumed incompetent unless they prove otherwise. This bias is literally our society's Achilles' heel perpetuating the talent and diversity gaps in technology, critical infrastructure, and its leadership.

It is about time that we address the elephant in the room. The way we educate, market to, employ, and "manage" girls and women needs a structural and fundamental overhaul. None of us can claim this is not our problem to solve.

Failure is not an option. Time is of the essence.

Where the Talent Gap Is Born

We have a supply shortage of cybersecurity talent. When you look at the supply chain as a funnel, the top of the funnel would be primary and secondary education. The middle represents college or university. The bottom is the workplace where professionals become part of the cybersecurity ecosystem. As you go through each stage, the funnel narrows dramatically. How?

Step 1: Primary and Secondary Education

The top of the funnel is a massive talent pool; limitless potential and lots of diversity! Primary and secondary education introduces technology and Internet-based applications to our children at an early age. It's the perfect time to introduce cybersecurity and privacy fundamentals. Yet schools do not teach students how to use the technology safely. Nor do they teach them how to protect their personal information, identity, intellectual property, or safety. Our educational system provides 21st-century technology with a 20th-century mindset. Blinders on!

If they introduce the concept of cybersecurity in a club or a CTE class (which is not very common), they represent it as a technical domain. This stuff is for the computer geeks who like to code or play video games. Do you see how we are losing interest in cybersecurity as a subject matter before kids have even decided what they want to be when they grow up? The system is already dismissing the path for most kids because we are compartmentalizing cybersecurity as a technology-only field. And within technology, we're assuming and sharing the assumption that coding is part of the curriculum no matter what you do in the cybersecurity workplace. Boy, are they wrong!

More often than not, cybersecurity as a possible learning opportunity or career path is not even mentioned to children in K-12. There are thousands of open jobs all over the world, but our educational system is not aware of them and is not preparing children to meet the demands of the future workplace. Not good.

Finally, there is a lack of diverse representation and role models who work in cybersecurity. There's a saying that *you can't be what you can't see.* We cannot expect young people to become cybersecurity professionals if they've never met any, let alone someone who looks like them and shares the same roots. Representation matters!

Step 2: Higher Education

Colleges and universities have developed cybersecurity programs over the years now. From associate's degrees in community colleges to bachelor's, master's, etc., in cybersecurity, there is no shortage anymore. Yet again, most focus on the technical aspect and ignore the importance of Governance, Risk, and Compliance (GRC) or fundamental cybersecurity practices around people and processes. By the way, hackers will more likely hack the person or the process than the technology. The MGM Casino hack in the fall of 2023 is a beautiful example of this.

As much as understanding the technology is important, we should expand the curriculum or even have degrees focused on additional skills: the administration of a cybersecurity program, the leadership skills needed to lead diverse technical teams, the communication and collaboration requirements within a business to build a cybersecurity culture. Most importantly, being able to relate cybersecurity risk to business risk and make cyber risk management a business function, funded and resourced as it should, are the ultimate lessons any aspiring cybersecurity professional and leader should learn. There is room for improvement and expansion whether in the cybersecurity or business curriculum.

It is important to note that there are many laws and regulations spanning states, countries, and regions worldwide that promote the privacy and security of their citizens, the protection of personal and sensitive information, and the resilience of critical infrastructure and supply chains. Privacy, i.e., the confidentiality of your personal information, will only grow in importance in a world where your images, videos, and personal information are plastered all over the Internet, and companies continue to monetize your data, your connections, and your attention, your eyeballs in marketing terms. That means that lawyers will become more and more involved in determining what a company's cybersecurity program looks like.

Step 3: The Workplace

When it comes to hiring cybersecurity professionals, something odd happens. Job descriptions are lengthy lists of requirements that no human being can meet. Hiring managers are looking for unicorns! Even junior or entry-level job roles require job experience (in years) and an education that is unrealistic. The big question is *why*?

It turns out that cybersecurity is managed by a small underfunded team and sometimes even one person, and when they have the luxury of hiring a new team member, they try to bundle the responsibilities of multiple roles all into one. On top of that, they don't have the time to train new hires because their hair is already on fire.

This is also the reason why cybersecurity internships are so few and far available, and you even have to apply in the fall the year before the summer you wish to work. It's like the Hunger Games!

It boils down to a lack of funding and executive support. Can't the latest software or AI silver bullet take care of it all? Can't we automate everything by now? Does it really have to be this complicated and expensive? Can't we do more with less?

The cybersecurity program you
want to run

The cybersecurity program you're
forced to run on your current budget

Did you know that Human Resources (HR) is a business function that is as underfunded and undervalued as IT and cybersecurity? This lack of resources and time in the people department results in a more reactive approach to hiring and people management. HR people don't speak cyber nor tech and don't necessarily understand what's involved in some of the certifications like a CISSP they add as a minimum requirement to an entry-level job description. While it would be easy to blame HR as they are publishing unattainable job postings, we need to recognize the common and underlying challenge HR and cybersecurity people face: a lack of executive support and financial commitment. Somewhere at the top where

strategy and organizational objectives are set, the people strategy is not
getting the support and resources it requires. If anything, people are seen
as a tremendous cost to the business, and when possible that's where the
cutting will happen first. Big mistake!

A by-product of unrealistic job postings is that you are immediately
and radically reducing your pool of job candidates. How? Turns out that
most women won't apply for a job unless they are confident they can
fill at least 80–90% of the job requirements. Why? Most women suffer
from this little thing called imposter syndrome. Go figure! Decades of the
world telling girls and women they are the helpers, the supporters, the
servants of men, incapable of doing men's work, is still an invisible voice
in their heads questioning whether they are capable or worthy of equal
opportunity (and equal pay), especially in "technical" and leadership
roles. This is partially why countless jobs cannot get filled. So many missed
opportunities on both sides of this equation!

Because of the workload and stress that any cybersecurity professional has to bear, retention of talent is becoming a real problem. The average tenure of a Chief Information Security Officer (CISO) is less than two years. Whenever a new CISO joins a company, a reset button is pressed, and progress may be lost. In addition, people with a more technical background are being promoted to leadership positions, where social, communication, and business management skills become more important than knowing the OSI model. This leads to misunderstandings and missed opportunities to improve the security posture and resilience of an organization.

The cybersecurity "talent gap" is the product of man-made systems gaps.

Lost in Translation

Cybersecurity has evolved over time as a function and responsibility within the Information Technology (IT) domain to its own function that encompasses people, processes, and technology. Cybersecurity is a responsibility of all people within an organization as it aims to ensure the Confidentiality, Integrity, and Availability of business-critical information and systems. We coin this the CIA triad.

- Human Resources has to perform background checks before they hire people. New hires need to sign an NDA, a cybersecurity Acceptable Use Policy (AUP) and receive cybersecurity awareness training on day one and on a recurring basis moving forward. When employees leave, proper offboarding procedures need to be followed.

- Procurement needs to include clauses in their agreements with vendors to protect the intellectual property of their organization and reduce their liability in case the vendor is affected by a breach.

- The leadership team needs to communicate their business objectives and strategic initiatives with the cybersecurity team, so they align their cybersecurity program objectives with the business goals. They are also responsible for setting a cybersecurity risk management strategy which the CISO executes.

- Software developers have to use secure software development lifecycle (SDLC) management practices. They have to embed privacy by design in any application that handles consumer or employee information or personal identifiable information (PII).

- Product management has to consult cybersecurity leadership before they develop a product to ensure they are secure by design.

- Finance has to implement dual roles and out-of-band verification processes to ensure they don't wire money to the wrong people.

- Sales and marketing have to be careful not to click a Request for Proposal (RFP) link or file from a "lead," i.e., an unknown person representing an unknown company.

- Even an intern needs to know that the CEO will not ask them for a gift card via email or text message.

However, many people leading organizations still see cybersecurity as another IT responsibility and a cost line item on their balance sheet. They don't understand that cybersecurity can be a business enabler, a way to build and grow trust with their clients and partners and a way to reduce business risk. They associate it like most of us to a technical field, and therefore a technical person has to take care of it.

Technical people however weren't taught how to talk to a CFO, COO, or CEO and how to make the business case for an investment in their cybersecurity program. They ask for money, and they never get it. The ROI is not there in the eyes of the executive leadership. Business leaders don't speak cyber or tech, and CISOs or security directors often don't speak the language of business or quantify risk in dollars and cents. They are lost in translation.

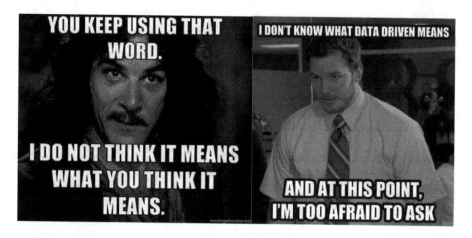

Bias in an Age of AI

Bias was an underlying reason why the CIA leadership and beyond weren't listening to the women who warned them about Osama Bin Laden and Al Qaeda well before 9/11. Bias is the underlying reason why our educational system gears STEM education to boys more than to girls. Bias will remain a fact of life. What's scarier, the technology that will be driving important decisions in our personal and professional lives may have biased algorithms. Big technology firms who want to dominate the world and keep growing their profits using artificial intelligence (AI) may amplify bias and create an even greater void between humans.

Social media, including Facebook, X, and YouTube, continue to monetize the distribution and consumption of content that propagates fear, uncertainty, and doubt (FUD) as those emotions keep users more engaged and that translates into more ad money. Such content may or may not be true and real. Now AI models used on the top of search engines are leveraging content shared on social media. Zero fact-checking.

If critical thinking is not part of the things we teach children and professionals alike, we will have little to no control over our own data and lives. If ethics is not a critical part of business leadership training or governance, technology may end up taking over, and we may be joining Neo in the battle against the Matrix, if we even realize we are in one. Do you want the red pill or the blue pill? Choose you must.

The only thing we have to fear is fear itself.

—Franklin D. Roosevelt

CHAPTER 5

How Does Cybercrime Affect You and Your Family?

Got Kids?

If you love your kids, you want them to be safe, right? Before you give them a mobile phone, gaming console, tablet, or laptop, teach yourself and them the basics on how to secure their identity, personal or sensitive information, and safety. Children are getting into serious trouble because of the gift of technology. Parents must understand that with great privilege comes great responsibility. It is no longer about looking both ways at a crosswalk or not talking to strangers who give out lollipops. It is about avoiding cybercriminals online. That's right; cybersecurity is about the safety of your kid.

© Cathy Olieslaeger 2025
C. Olieslaeger, *Cybersecurity for Everyone*, Apress Pocket Guides,
https://doi.org/10.1007/979-8-8688-1408-2_5

Got Parents?

Here's the sad reality. The elderly are as much targeted by scammers as our children. They too have crossed the bridge to digital communications and are struggling to wrap their heads around the ever-changing technology. They don't understand that there are so many bad actors in every corner of the world looking to make a buck on grandma's or grandpa's back, very often over the phone. They desperately need your help.

The annual Internet Crime Report published by the FBI in 2024 talks about the dramatic increase in impersonation scams that include government and tech/customer support impersonation. The financial losses in one year amount to a whopping $1.3 billion representing 51,750 complaints with the IC3. Almost half of the complainants (40%) were over 60 years old but ended up losing 58% of the total losses.

This Cannot Happen to You? Think Again

We all have some degree of awareness of the dark side of the Internet. Cybercrime organizations leverage the latest hacks and tools available on the dark web for a few bucks. They can purchase personal information from millions of people and create a massive email campaign, combined with calls, messaging via mobile, social media, gaming consoles, Discord or Telegram forums, you name it, and armed with generative AI, botnets, and automation, the scale and speed of their hacks increase exponentially. They never cease to adapt to innovative detection and attack strategies, always finding new ways to hack their targets. Nobody is off limits. Nobody is safe.

Here are a few strategies that could fool the best of us:

- (S)extortion using real or AI-generated fake images and videos

- Charity scams

- Disinformation campaigns during elections

- Cryptocurrency investment schemes

- Fake lawyers offering services to victims of cryptocurrency scams to help recover stolen funds

- LinkedIn scams

- Fake online university and college degree scams

- Student loan scams

- Real estate wire fraud

Why?

There is a wide variety of ways people of all ages are being targeted, manipulated, hacked, and hurt on the Internet. Between gaming, social media, streaming, dating, and communication platforms, the opportunities to take advantage of people's innocence or ignorance are endless. The important question to ask is *why*? Why would anyone target your kids, your parents, and everyone in between? To what end?

Cybercriminals are very opportunistic, and they are often driven by financial motives, less than destructive motives. But in today's volatile geopolitical world, cyberwarfare is rampant, and we may be casualties of war or pawns in a quest for more power. The two may also overlap; cybercrime syndicates may be funding the wars waged by their autocratic regimes they live under. In order to operate their cybercrime business, they must bend the knee and kiss the ring.

Financial Objectives

Your Data Is Not Yours to Keep

If the product is free, you are the product. What does that mean? Personal information, likes, dislikes, images, and videos are posted on social media. Companies like Meta (Facebook, Instagram, etc.), Alphabet (Google, YouTube, etc.), TikTok, X (formerly known as Twitter), etc., are collecting this information and monetizing it, all of it. On one hand, they are selling it to data brokers who continue to sell it to others. They are also selling advertisers these very detailed profiles, even psychological profiles, so ads can be tailored to the individual. On the other hand, they are feeding their artificial intelligence engines with all this data, so they can sell AI technology.

These organizations are very powerful corporations, and their lobbyists have kept US lawmakers from regulating them as much as the European Union has. In the European Union, EU citizens have far more privacy rights than Americans. The GDPR has implemented the Right to be Forgotten, which gives the EU citizens the right to request to have their accounts and all data collected to be deleted. In the United States, you can subscribe to services to help delete your information, but it won't stop organizations from collecting and trading your data the next day.

Data Brokers

Data brokers who hoard and resell vast amounts of data on people worldwide become prime hacking targets. Why hack thousands of people or organizations if you only need to hack one data broker? That's exactly what happened to National Public Data, a Florida data broker that lost around 300 million of social security numbers and other personally identifiable information (PII) in a data breach. Let that sink in: 300 million people were affected in one hack! That's almost the entire US population.

Data brokers collect information that's readily available through public records and may include

- Bankruptcies

- Census data

- Court records

- Criminal history

- Insurance

- Liens

- Motor vehicle records

- Property information

- Voter registration information

Public records could also include demographic information about

- Where you live

- Your age

- Your employment history

- Names and ages of your family

- Names of people you have direct relationships with

- Whether you have been married or divorced

When Data Collection Turns into Surveillance and Harm

The whereabouts of our mobile phones can now be constantly tracked by all the applications we use. But some organizations take this data and monetize it to allow for individual or mass surveillance of the device and its movement. An average person would call this spyware.

For example, Krebs on Security shared in October of 2024 an article on a class action case led by Atlas against Babel Street, an organization accused of not following "Daniel's Law, a New Jersey statute allowing law enforcement, government personnel, judges and their families to have their information completely removed from commercial data brokers. Daniel's Law was passed in 2020 after the death of 20-year-old Daniel Anderl, who was killed in a violent attack targeting a federal judge — his mother."

Babel Street's offering allows its clients to isolate and monitor individual phones, tracking people's movements which was used to threaten law enforcement officers' lives. It isn't hard to imagine how this technology at the hands of extremist groups could lead to harm.

The article continues to broaden the picture beyond one organization. "Babel Street re-hosts data from the commercial phone tracking firm Venntel. The U.S. Federal Trade Commission has opened an inquiry into Venntel and its parent company Gravy Analytics. Venntel has also been a data partner of the police surveillance contractor Fog Data Science, whose product has been described as 'mass surveillance on a budget.'"

"Atlas alleges that in response to requests to have data on its New Jersey law enforcement clients scrubbed from consumer records sold by LexisNexis, the data broker retaliated by freezing the credit of approximately 18,500 people, and falsely reporting them as identity theft victims. In addition, Atlas said LexisNexis started returning failure codes indicating they had no record of these individuals, resulting in denials when officers attempted to refinance loans or open new bank accounts."

Clearly, the boundaries around our data privacy are very blurred, and a vast ecosystem is in the business of violating it at the possible expense of our safety.

Data Breaches

Your data is collected by a lot of organizations, including your employer, doctor, accountant, bank, credit card, insurance provider, etc. Some types of data are more valuable than others. Here are a few ways your data may end up being stolen during a data breach.

Healthcare Data

Your health records include a lot of your personal information beyond the typical personal identifiable information (PII). They have a greater street value on the dark web than most other types of records. So it pays to hack hospitals and their business associates; ransomware attacks have historically paid off royally. Hospitals and their business associates have to meet the HIPAA Security and Privacy protection rules. Not meeting these requirements and still falling victim to a security breach may result in fines. On top of the cost to the people whose records have been stolen, hospitals are facing high costs related to cybercrime and its aftermath. Maybe this adds to the inflation of healthcare costs we have been witnessing in recent years?

As required by section 13402(e)(4) of the HITECH Act, the Office for Civil Rights (OCR) within the US Department of Health and Human Services posts a list of breaches of unsecured protected health information affecting 500 or more individuals. You can visit this on the website, often referred to as "the wall of shame," below:

https://ocrportal.hhs.gov/ocr/breach/breach_report.jsf

A few noteworthy breaches in healthcare and beyond:

- **Change Healthcare, Inc.**: In early 2024, Change Healthcare, a UnitedHealth subsidiary, was the target of a ransomware attack that disrupted payment processing and health services. The US Department of

Health and Human Services confirmed that 100 million people were impacted, making it one of the largest breaches of medical and health data in US history.

- **23andMe**: A hacker used stolen usernames and passwords to log in and view account information, including health data. Through the platform's DNA Relatives or Family Tree profile service, the hacker obtained additional information on relatives of the account owners they breached. In total, 23andMe said in a class action settlement that 6.4 million people in the United States had information downloaded by the hacker.

- **NHS**: The UK's National Health Service had 16 breaches that exposed 1.8 million health records during the 12-month period ending in July 2012. Up until now, NHS has been the target of ransomware attacks, including one on a provider called Synnovis in June of 2024 by a Russian gang called Qilin. This affected operations at multiple hospitals across London.

All this data is stolen either to sell it to other crooks or to commit identity theft. Identity theft can have an effect on you when someone who uses your identity...

- Commits a crime and now you have a criminal record

- Opens a credit card and now you have to pay the bill

- Gets into a car accident and now your car insurance cost goes through the roof

- Goes to the hospital and gets medical treatment under your insurance and you receive the invoice which you can't afford to pay

Your credit score gets ruined by any of these events that affect your wallet. So when you apply for a job, a mortgage, a car loan, a credit card, or college scholarship, you get denied. Your life comes to a complete halt.

Credit Card Data

The Payment Card Industry (PCI) is governed worldwide by a collection of credit card companies (Visa, Mastercard, American Express, Discover). Your credit card data should be stored and transmitted in encrypted format to keep it secure by organizations who take or process credit card payments. Yet scammers continue to target your credit card information, so they can shop 'til they drop and leave you holding the check – whether by targeting retailers, hotels, travel sites, restaurants, their business partners, etc., or by placing card skimmers on or near credit card payment terminals or ATMs.

A few noteworthy PCI-related breaches:

- **Equifax**: Over 143 million Americans, or 45% of the US population at the time, as well as Canadian and UK citizens were affected. The data lost included social security numbers, birth dates, addresses, driver's licenses, and credit card numbers.

- **Heartland Payment Systems**: They process payment card transactions for 175,000 merchants, including many banks, and was breached via SQL injection in 2008. Over 134 million credit cards were compromised.

While most big name stores, restaurant chains, hotels, etc., have likely been the target and victim of these types of hacks, because of the strong enforcement of the PCI standard, the collective defenses of credit card data has improved.

Even though organizations have invested heavily in the protection of credit card holder data, their focus has been often myopic and left the rest of their organization vulnerable to a variety of cyber threats. Ransomware, extortion, credential stuffing, supply chain attacks, and destructive wiper malware have expanded the potential impact to the organizations and the people they serve.

Extortion

On the flip side of the publicly traded mega tech corporations, those lovely unicorns that take and sell your data are private organizations operating under the radar, but with serious funding, resources, and resolve to make a big buck. These shady organizations are looking to extort money from people they are engaged with through social or gaming platforms' messaging offerings (WhatsApp, Messenger, Discord, Telegram, X, etc.). People are "befriended," and, without ever meeting, trust is built by playing on sensitive topics and emotions. They may use voice cloning or even deep fake video technology to hide their own identities. Extortion schemes targeting young, single, elderly, and other individuals are rampant. As long as the awareness and education around these social engineering tactics are not being taught with the introduction of technology to people, young and old, the hackers will continue to win.

Cryptocurrency Hacks

A continuation from some of the abovementioned social engineering ploys are cryptocurrency schemes. The lure of lucrative investments has moved into the cryptocurrency domain, and people befriended over the Internet are "offered" a great opportunity to participate in a once-in-a-lifetime crypto investment. Our tendency to be polite or nice sometimes overrides our common-sense ability to say "no" to social engineers who know exactly what to say whenever you are questioning their proposal. If it sounds too good to be true, it is not true. Trust your gut.

Summary

The short lesson is that your data is not yours. Your data is the new oil. Someone plans to make a lot of money with it, one way or another, legally or not, whether you like it or not. And if that isn't enough, extortion or cryptocurrency investment scams using well-developed playbooks are used to extort and bankrupt people. The ultimate threat is when your data is turned into a weapon against you and your family, virtually or physically.

Your data, your identity, and your safety all go hand in hand. To protect one, you must protect all. You do control to some degree what technology and applications you use, what data you share, whom you befriend on social media, and whether you allow your children and elderly parents on social platforms. You do have the right and ability to talk to your representatives and lobby for better privacy protection laws and a greater level of accountability for those who violate your privacy. Not to discount all the bad things all the bad guys do, you do have some control in this matter.

Change or Influence Behavior

What drives our behavior? Why do we do what we do? Very often, we are driven by fear, uncertainty, and doubt (FUD) more than reason. The fear of missing out (FOMO) or the fear of not being liked or included is an emotion played on by those who wish to influence our behavior.

Anyone studying marketing has learned about the power of influence and persuasion. Robert Cialdini's Principles of Persuasion are the foundation of all marketing ploys used worldwide, good and bad. The principles that drive people to say YES include

- **Reciprocity**: If someone gives you a gift, a favor, or a compliment, now you owe them. You are more likely to do something for someone if they gave you something first.

- **Scarcity**: Someone may want you to act fast or buy a product by making it less available or at a discounted price during a limited period of time.

- **Authority**: We are more likely to listen to and trust people who have authority or seem to have it either by title, by wearing a uniform, or by acting like they own the place.

- **Commitment and consistency**: We are more likely to say yes to a request if we believe it is consistent with our previous actions or identity.

- **Liking**: We are more likely to be persuaded by someone we like.

- **Consensus or social proof**: We are more likely to buy a product or act a certain way if we witness others doing it first. In a world of influencers, we know how this works, right?

- **Unity**: People are more likely to participate in an activity if they feel included.

The need to belong and to fit in continues to affect our behavior online and beyond. People gravitate to people who look, act, and talk like them. The risk of not having diversity in your environment is groupthink. Groupthink values harmony and coherence over accurate analysis and critical thinking of individual members. It creates a group where individual members of the group are unable to express their own thoughts and concerns and unquestioningly follow the word of the leader.

Irving Janis identifies the following eight symptoms of groupthink:

- Invulnerability

- Rationale

- Morality

- Stereotypes

- Pressure

- Self-censorship

- Illusion of unanimity

- Mind guards

In short, a group of people build a tunnel vision and don't allow dissent within their group. To belong, you must follow, blindly and quietly. Led by someone with ulterior motives, you may be doing the dirty work for them and suffer the consequences sooner or later.

The impact of groupthink can be small or very large scale. A few examples where groupthink was at play:

- The dotcom bubble when every startup with dotcom at the end of their name was given a blank check and never made it past the first year of their existence. The 2000 stock market crash was a direct result of the bursting of the dotcom bubble. It popped when a majority of the technology startups that raised money and went public folded when capital ran out.

- The housing bubble and financial crisis in 2007–2008 when banks gave away variable interest rate mortgages to people who couldn't afford them (subprime mortgages), especially when interest rates went up, and sold the mortgages to investors as collateralized debt obligations.

- US intelligence agencies run by mostly men in suits did not pay attention to the warnings around Osama Bin Laden by the women of Alec Station, the anti-terrorism organization within the CIA, ultimately not being able to prevent the 9/11/2001 attacks in the United States.

- Cryptocurrency, which in many cases is not backed by anything of value, has seen major spikes in recent years. Collectively, crypto investors expect a continued upward trend in the crypto market. Let's see how that goes.

Retail and Hospitality

The retail and hospitality industry know exactly which buttons to press to make you press the Buy or Reserve Now buttons. They master the art of persuasion. They urge people to act fast, or they will miss out on lots of savings even though their bank account cannot afford another purchase of an unnecessary gadget or experience.

Have you noticed how advertisements pop up on your phone, social media, streaming platforms, and so on based on your Internet browsing or searching activities or even after you were talking to someone about a product? Not only are they now customizing their advertisements based on more information they collect from you (with or without your consent), they are also more pervasive across all digital platforms you operate on. There is no hiding from them, is there?

Playbook of Dictators, Past and Present

Persuasion is not limited to the art of the deal. The use of propaganda and controlling the narrative was and continues to be a page from the dictator's playbook. They may even use the "Freedom of Speech" premise to promote messages that are unfounded or untrue. What dictatorships and authoritarian regimes have taught us is that the best way to mass-manipulate people is to limit or censor their news sources and control the narrative elsewhere.

Nazi Germany in the 1930s and 1940s is a prime example of censorship and propaganda which played an integral role in advancing the persecution and ultimately the genocide of Europe's Jews. It incited hatred and fostered a climate of indifference to their fate. Germans simply claimed "Befehl ist Befehl" or "Orders are Orders" in an effort to avoid accountability for their actions.

Autocracies in today's world are implementing the same practices. Countries like China, Russia, North Korea, and Iran control their Internet platforms and block certain news or social media platforms so their citizens only hear and see what their government tells them and don't share the injustices they may be facing at the hands of autocratic leaders.

The lure of power and the need to gain more and more of it are not unique to a handful of autocrats in foreign countries on continents far away. The political theater in every corner of the world has mastered the use of messages to move people to choose, vote, and act in certain ways that benefit the ultimate winner of power. The question is are these messages factual, accurate, and reliable or are they disinformation meant to play on our emotions and sway our vote in one direction or another?

As long as the business model of social media and content platforms continues to rely on income from advertisements, these questions remain unanswered, and blindly trusting any content shared on them would be a serious mistake.

An example is Cambridge Analytica which collected massive amounts of information from over 50 million users on Facebook, developed psychological profiles, and then tailored advertisements to discredit Hillary Clinton as presidential candidate and help Donald Trump win in the 2016 US election.

Whether it is the elections in the United States, Europe, or other regions, some powerful autocracies may prefer one outcome over the other, so they can continue implementing their own political agenda which may include the annexation of neighboring territories or sovereign states. The war waged on the Ukraine, which started with cyberattacks on their electric grid by the way, is an example why the Russian state has been causing so much political disruption within the United States and NATO countries. As long as they are distracted with their internal discourse and grievances, Russia can continue their brutal and lethal transgressions. China has been eyeing Hong Kong and Taiwan, Israel has been leveling Gaza and Lebanon, and North Korea has been growing its long-range missile program, just to name a few.

In a world connected by the Internet and where economies depend on a global supply chain, these violations of human rights, destruction of cities and civil infrastructure, and the compromise of a nation's sovereignty end up affecting people everywhere one way or another. The short-term result is inflation; things get more expensive. Natural gas prices and therefore heating costs skyrocketed in Europe when part two of the Russia-Ukraine war erupted in 2022.

China has spent decades infiltrating organizations across many regions not only to extract intellectual property to reduce their R&D costs and produce cheaper products to gain a massive competitive edge, making them a very powerful supplier to the rest of the world for almost everything. They have also infiltrated critical infrastructure such as utilities providing water or energy to millions of people as a deterrent strategy to keep countries like the United States from intervening when they make their next power grab move.

One important question you must ask: How are these wars at the hands of autocrats funded? The short answer is ransomware. Ransomware is a type of malware that encrypts all digital records within an organization; the hackers demand a ransom payment in Bitcoin, which in many cases gets paid. Healthcare organizations have been prime targets worldwide. Bitcoin is then used to buy weapons and bombs that are dropped on hospitals in Ukraine and beyond. It is beyond cruel; it is evil. Cybercrime affects people in the virtual and physical world. It is one piece of the puzzle, an important chapter in the power-hungry autocrat's playbook.

As long as autocracies prevail, cybercrime and the steep cost thereof will continue to affect all of us. Per CISA's Director Jen Easterly's words, a threat to one is a threat to all. Cybersecurity is national security.

> *When the power of love overcomes the love of power, the world will know peace.*
>
> —Jimi Hendrix

From Terrorism to Extreme Politics

Terrorist or extremist organizations like ISIS have developed a playbook of their own on how to convert law-abiding individuals, even children, into radicalized terrorists. A 2017 United Nations report on the recruitment of children by terrorist or extremist organizations explains, "As active Internet users, children are at particular risk. Specific websites advertise the existence of the groups and, in many instances, multiple sites in different languages include different messages tailored to specific audiences. Social media platforms, including email, chat rooms, e-groups, message boards, video recordings and applications are especially popular recruitment tools that can also facilitate tailored approaches. One of the methods, which can be defined as "grooming", is based on the perpetrator learning about the individual's interests in order to tailor the approach and build up a relationship of trust. A second technique replicates "targeted advertising": by tracking the online behavior of Internet users, a group can identify those vulnerable to its propaganda and tailor the narrative to suit its target audience." When it comes to the propaganda techniques, "Cartoons and computer games and other interactive media appearing on the Internet have been designed to appeal to children in particular. Often colourful content is integrated within material that glorifies terrorist acts, including suicide attacks."

Turning people into violent pawns is not limited to terrorist organizations hiding in caves. This threat is everywhere, whether the puppeteer is in Russia operating massive botnets or in the heartland of the United States. And they have access to the largest mind control platforms worldwide.

In a 2018 PBS Frontline documentary on New American Nazis, such as Atomwaffen, it shows how social media plays a role in propagating hate and inciting young men to take violent actions against people, critical infrastructure, and synagogues. It also documents how it targets men in the military to join their cause. White power activism is actively recruiting, grooming, and driving the behaviors of young men and military members using social platforms. Given the removal of any oversight on social media platforms, this threat of violence from within will grow unchecked. Extreme right organizations whether underground or above are gaining popularity not only in the United States but in Europe since social media has no geographical boundaries.

The January 6, 2021, riot and deadly violence in Washington, DC, was fueled on social media platforms which allowed disinformation to be spread about the presidential election results and the encouragement to take violent action. Per *Washington Post* article on the involvement of social media before, during, and after this historic violent event, "In the days before Jan. 6, 2021, media reports documented Trump's call on Twitter for people to rally in Washington — it'll be wild, he tweeted — and there was growing talk of guns and potential violence on sites such as Telegram, Parler and TheDonald.win."

"The Purple Team's memo detailed how the actions of roughly 15 social networks played a significant role in the attack. It described how major platforms like Facebook and Twitter, prominent video streaming sites like YouTube and Twitch and smaller fringe networks like Parler, Gab and 4chan served as megaphones for those seeking to stoke division or organize the insurrection. It detailed how some platforms bent their rules to avoid penalizing conservatives out of fear of reprisals, while others were reluctant to curb the "Stop the Steal" movement after the attack."

The people who stormed the Capitol, which included many members of extreme militia groups, truly believed that democracy was ending if Donald Trump didn't become President again, as they believed him and others who claimed his victory. So they followed orders and did what they thought was right. Hundreds of them landed in jail, some because they ruthlessly killed Capitol police officers. They were the perpetrators of a coup d'état.

In his third bid for the US Presidency in 2024, it was of no surprise that Donald Trump not only used his own social platform, Truth Social, but became very close to Elon Musk, CEO of X, a.k.a. Twitter. This widened the reach of his messaging, including disinformation campaigns that went unchecked.

This and many violent events are why the FBI and Department of Homeland Security have reported that a growing threat to the United States is the threat from domestic terrorists. We have become our own worst enemy, unbeknownst to ourselves.

> *Our lives begin to end the day we become silent about things that matter.*
>
> —Martin Luther King, Jr.

Summary

We are human and therefore we are vulnerable to social engineering and manipulation efforts that may influence our behaviors. This may be a long-term, subliminal, and subtle campaign that sways our opinions, feelings, and ultimately our actions years down the road. Being aware of the threats that lurk on social media is absolutely critical. Whether you continue to use these platforms is a choice. What is the risk versus reward equation to you?

It is also important to understand the bigger picture. Elections are being influenced as it may benefit autocracies on other continents. The bounty of cybercrime may fuel terrorism or wars. And as the dust settles, the financial impact can be felt worldwide. Inflation is the boomerang effect from cybercrime and wars funded by ransomware. One way or another, we deal with the aftermath.

Knowledge is Power

—Francis Bacon

Are You Part of the Solution or Part of the Problem?

The frontline in cyber is human. We are all connected to each other whether in our personal or professional relations. You may be a target because of who you are related to. You may just be the backdoor to the next person or organization. It is easier to fool a person than to bypass the technology and its sophisticated defenses. The bad guys are winning, and the more they win, the more they'll keep doing it. It will not only remain a reality but it will get worse if we don't increase our awareness and education of good cyber hygiene and simple best practices. You and I, we are in this together. Are you ready to be part of the solution?

If you can dream it, you can do it.

—Walt Disney

CHAPTER 6

How to Keep You and Your Family Safe

Password Manager

Forget about coming up with unique long passwords for every single application you use at home or at work. I know it is impossible to remember them. Many people still reuse the same password over and over again. And very often your password will include your pet's name, favorite sports team, birthday (all the things you share on social media), or 123456789. Do you really believe that is good enough?

The solution is to use a password manager and let that generate, update, and store your passwords securely. The most important thing is to secure your password manager with two things, nothing more and nothing less. One, use a passphrase instead of a password to protect access to it. This is something you – and only you – know. Two, use a second authentication code as another step to gain access to your password manager or vault. This is something you have. Combined, we call that 2-factor authentication.

© Cathy Olieslaeger 2025
C. Olieslaeger, *Cybersecurity for Everyone*, Apress Pocket Guides,
https://doi.org/10.1007/979-8-8688-1408-2_6

Password managers can be applications you download on your mobile phone, tablet, and computer. Do your research to see which password manager is recommended in the industry. In three years after this book is published, that may be a different solution than today, so do your homework.

A few examples currently available:

- Bitwarden

- 1Password

- Dashlane

WIRED published an article on the best password managers they recommend in April 2024. They recommend some of the password managers above, among others, but explicitly did not recommend LastPass anymore, citing the multiple security breaches they had suffered. Any technology or organization that collects a lot of sensitive data from a lot of people or other organizations has a big target on their virtual backs. This may be why passwords will be a thing of the past in the near future.

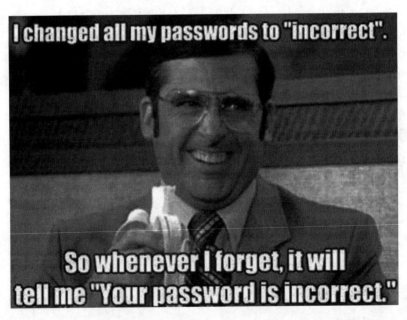

Passphrase

What is the difference between a password and a passphrase? First, a passphrase should be longer than a password. It is a sentence that should include lower and upper case letters, numbers, and special characters, at least 12 characters long. It can be a title of a book, a line in a song or poem, or a random combination of words that only make sense to you, with the addition of some random numbers and characters, so it is impossible to guess even with some of the more sophisticated password crackers. The key is that it has a lot of characters; the longer, the better.

An example: "In2023MyDogAteMyDonut!"

If you want to do even better, use the first letters of the words in a passphrase to create a password with no words at all. WhenHarryMetSally@theDinerinNYCin1989 becomes "WHMS@ tDiNYCi1898".

Two-Factor Authentication

However, did you know that bad actors may also install spyware on your devices that collect your keystrokes? These key loggers could easily steal your passwords or passphrases, no matter how complex. For that reason and because of the common exploitation of stolen credentials, you need a second factor or code generated on a device that you have on hand.

Two-factor authentication (2FA) or multifactor authentication (MFA) comes in various types. 2FA using SMS or texting a code is a commonly used method. Because it is so widely used, it also became a hacking target and something that can be hacked now. Those darn hackers just keep pushing the boundaries! The best practice is now to use an authenticator application on a mobile phone. Microsoft, Google, and others give you free access to their authenticator app. All you need to do is activate 2FA on whichever application you use by scanning a QR code with your mobile phone's authenticator app. Again, do your research and ensure the app is widely used and has been vetted before you download it.

Yubico is an organization that offers the YubiKey. This device acts like a physical key to your computer or mobile phone. It allows you to authenticate to any application using the YubiKey for MFA. Even if a hacker has access to your password, without physically having access to your YubiKey, a bad actor won't be able to access your account.

The Future Is Passwordless

That's right; the days of us using passwords are numbered. This is a direct consequence of people using the same password for everything and their email accounts at work being hacked. It is also because most people use weak passwords that are easily guessable or cracked and again their email gets hacked.

When a work email gets hacked, and a business email compromise (BEC) leads to the propagation of malware, an organization can suffer substantial financial losses due to the replacement cost of hardware, the incident response process, and the aftermath from fines and lawsuits. This cost turns into increased prices to customers. It can and has led to bankruptcy which leads to people losing their jobs. Do you see why this matters to you now?

So what does a passwordless solution look like? It will require people to authenticate themselves using a physical interface on their device. Time to become familiar with passkeys as Microsoft has recently announced that they will make one billion users of their Office solutions away from passwords.

Biometrics

You are already familiar with one solution: the use of your biometrics such as the scan of your fingerprint or your face.

Passkeys

Fast Identity Online (FIDO) is an open standard for passwordless authentication. FIDO allows users and organizations to leverage the standard to sign in to their resources using an external security key or a platform key built into a device, eliminating the need for a username and password.

These FIDO security keys are typically USB devices, but could also be Bluetooth or Near Field Communication (NFC)–based devices, which are used for short-range wireless data transfer. With a hardware device that handles the authentication, the security of an account is increased as there's no password that could be stolen or guessed.

Apple and Microsoft support FIDO and named them passkeys. Passkeys are generated cryptographic keys managed by your device (usually your phone). Your phone-generated passkeys are stored on your device and usually protected by either biometrics or PINs. Since passkeys are generated key pairs instead of passwords, there's nothing to remember.

The sooner you adopt passkeys, the harder of a hacking target you become.

Be Aware of Social Engineering

Social engineering keeps evolving and takes on different approaches. It is no longer an email that looks phishy (phishing). It can be a text message (smishing) from someone you know, a message on your Facebook Messenger app from your friend, or a chat in a gaming chat room or on Discord. It can also be a voice message or call (vishing). It won't be long until your image and voice will be used in widespread AI-generated impersonation attacks. The possibilities to hack a human are literally endless.

The ultimate goal of social engineering is to infect your device and/or network with malware. Malware comes in all kinds of shapes and sizes. It can be embedded in websites that a URL points to, files shared electronically, mobile apps, and even pictures. It can worm itself into systems without you interacting with it. It can change its signature, so it cannot be detected. It can hide its tracks, so it is harder to determine its trajectory and motives. There are millions of malware strains being released on any given day. Malware can encrypt, extract, or wipe your data, record video from your webcam, listen in on your conversations from your microphone, collect your keystrokes and passwords, destroy your device turning it inoperable, and allow hackers to take over your drives, email, social media, banking, online retail accounts, and so forth and so on. And then they move on to the next person.

In cybersecurity, we now use the concept of Zero Trust. We assume that the user or an organization has already been compromised and that the bad actor is already among us. We say, it is not a matter of if, but when, someone gets hacked. There is no illusion about it anymore; humans will be compromised one way or another. There are those who know they've been hacked and those who don't know it yet. You absolutely must have the same Zero Trust attitude toward your personal connections and the technology they use.

What Would You Do for Love?

Online dating is our modern day way of finding our next true love, the soulmate we've all been dreaming of. But you should know that this is the perfect place to be fooled and robbed. *Pig butchering* is no joke! Men and women, even some who work in cybersecurity, have fallen in love and then got robbed blind in a blink of an eye. You may not believe it, but the Nigerian Prince email scammers have moved on to the big business of crypto scams and broken hearts. If someone whom you never met in person, but you've been chatting online for months now, is suggesting on a WhatsApp channel to invest in this crypto investment that sounds too good to be true, *it is too good to be true.* You know better! But for love, we may just give it a try, right?

Young teenagers are also getting into all kinds of trouble in the dark world of cyber. *Sextortion* is affecting more and more children (and adults), and this is tragically resulting in suicide in some cases and the complete devastation of families. Do not underestimate the technical savviness of your children nor the dark corners of the applications they are using every day. Social media is a darker place than you may think. You absolutely need to speak openly about these dangers with your loved ones, whether they're your children, parents, friends, or colleagues. None of us are immune to these dangers as soon and as long as we are using the Internet and in particular social media.

Predators use social media not only to befriend someone and execute a financial extortion scheme. They can also use pictures posted on social media or metadata collected by social media to locate your physical presence. Some applications allow people to see profiles of friends of friends, again gaining access to minors and their information, potentially their location.

Human trafficking is a by-product of unsafe social media and technology use. Sadly, this is another practice that is growing exponentially. "A total of 2,027 persons were referred to U.S. attorneys for human trafficking offenses in fiscal year 2021, a 49% increase from the 1,360 persons referred in 2011," as reported by the Bureau of Justice Statistics.

As much as your heart wants to find love or just a friend, do not trust people you meet online. Hard stop.

There are many resources now available to teach your children about online safety and how to deal with these threats when they become a reality. These include videos and cartoons to make it a bit easier for them to digest.

- Secure our World, How to Keep your Family Safe, CISA

  - https://www.cisa.gov/secure-our-world

- How to help families keep children safe online, eSafety, Australia's independent regulator for online safety

  - https://www.esafety.gov.au/communities/child-safe-communities/families

- Resources on how to manage sextortion

  - https://www.missingkids.org/theissues/sextortion#resources

Double-Check

When in doubt, even if there is no doubt, follow these steps to ensure authenticity and protect yourself from scams:

- Always call the person directly using the phone number you have saved on your phone to check that it was truly them who emailed, texted, or shared something with you.

- Voice cloning and even the use of avatars and your likeness using pictures or videos found on the Internet are being used to imitate someone and manipulate you to act against your own best interest. Call a person on the number you have on record if you receive an upsetting voicemail or call sounding like a loved one who is asking for financial help.

- Develop a two-step process that helps you authenticate your close circle like your parents, siblings, and children. Use a code or question and answer that only you know to confirm you are you and they are who they claim to be.

71

- Scams may also sound like legitimate calls or outreach from law enforcement, the government like the IRS, or financial institutions. Never take any of these calls or messages seriously until you find a way to confirm their origin and intent. Call 911, your local police station, your bank, or the IRS to check whether the call, voicemail, email, or message you received was indeed sent from their office.

Don't call, text, or email the person back. If there is a serious sense of urgency, your internal red flags and alarm bells should be raised and blaring. Stay calm and check before you start to panic and act irrationally. Assume a Zero Trust attitude and say: "It's just another scammer looking to make a quick buck. Not today!"

Report

Just like you would call the police when you see someone breaking into your neighbor's house, or the fire department when there's a house on fire in your neighborhood, you must report cybercrimes, so cybercriminals can be traced and locked up. If we don't stop them, they will not stop.

In the United States, you can report cybercrimes or online scams with local police departments as well as the Internet Crime Complaint Center (IC3) operated by the FBI. They may be able to connect the dots of multiple crimes, identify, and capture the cybercriminals.

The benefit of you reporting cybercrime will not only benefit the greater good, there is also a chance that the FBI can assist in stopping the flow of money so it doesn't reach the cybercriminal. IC3's Recovery Asset Team (RAT), established in 2018, streamlines communications with financial institutions and FBI field offices to facilitate the freezing of funds for victims. In 2023, IC3's RAT initiated the Financial Fraud Kill

Chain (FFKC) on 3,008 incidents, with potential losses of $758.05 million. A monetary hold was placed on $538.39 million, representing a success rate of 71%.

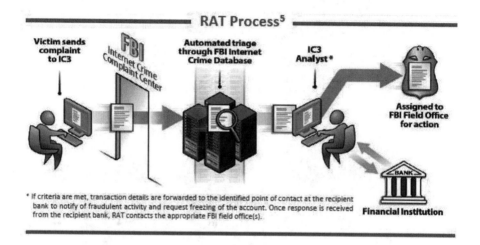

Update Software and Hardware

I hope it is no mystery anymore that you have to update your phone, laptop, or computer with the most recent operating system, malware protection, or other software versions, including your web browser as soon as these updates or patches are released. Updates exist to keep your technology secure.

However, you may have more Internet-connected devices in your home, car, office, and beyond than you realize. They too need to be updated as soon as you install them and from that day forward. First, you need to update the default password, then ensure the device updates itself automatically whenever an update is available. If your latest gadget lacks that capability, maybe you want to think twice about that purchase and definitely before you connect it to your home or business Wi-Fi network.

Freeze Your Credit

In the United States, people are equated to a number. Their entire lives, Americans are monitored and controlled by every major institution using their social security number which is issued at birth. You have to share your social security number for every financial transaction: from opening a bank account, signing up for a credit card, when needing a car loan or a home mortgage, receiving healthcare, attending college, and getting a job. Your worth or value in the eyes of these institutions is determined by the credit score that is reported by three credit agencies. That score reflects your ability to pay off your loans and bills on time among other factors. It answers the question: Can they trust you?

The best and only way to prevent identity theft or someone messing up your credit or FICO score is to freeze your credit. This is assuming your personal identifiable information (PII), especially your social security number, has already been compromised. Honestly, you would be extremely lucky if your data hasn't yet been stolen and then sold on the dark web. So assume compromise and have a Zero Trust attitude when it comes to your data.

The three organizations holding the power over your credit worthiness are Experian, TransUnion, and Equifax. And guess what!? They too have already been breached and lost your precious personal data in recent years. Isn't that ironic?

What does it mean to freeze your credit? To freeze your credit means that you block access to your data associated with your social security number and only if you unfreeze it can it be used to request a line of credit.

Each organization has a process for you to create an account and freeze your credit. How do they know it's you? They will know things like all the addresses you've ever lived at, the types of cars you owned, and who your employers were, for example. And after a few multiple-choice questions, they will determine whether or not you are you. The sooner you do this, the better as so much of your personal information is already being gathered by other data hoarding organizations who sell it to the highest bidders!

How to contact the credit agencies to request a credit freeze:

Equifax
PO Box 105788
Atlanta, GA 30348
1-800-349-9960
https://www.equifax.com/personal/credit-report-services/
credit-freeze/

Experian
PO Box 9554
Allen, TX 75013
1-888-397-3742
https://www.experian.com/freeze/center.html

TransUnion
PO Box 2000
Chester, PA 19016
1-888-909-8872
https://www.transunion.com/credit-freeze

When you freeze your credit, the credit agency will send you confirmation of the placement of the freeze along with information on how to remove the freeze, including any authentication information you will need, such as a personal identification number (PIN) or password. The information should be sent to you no later than five business days after placing the freeze.

Make sure to keep any authentication information in a safe place, like a password manager that is protected with a long passphrase and 2FA using an authenticator app, or in a physical safe.

Protect Your Privacy

There are a few ways you can protect your privacy online. This domain will evolve over time, but it will require people to put more pressure on their local legislators and state representatives in Washington, DC. As long as big corporations are beefing up their back pockets, your rights may be secondary to their own interests. Use your vote wisely.

- Read the Terms of Service (TOS) before you accept them. Don't accept them especially when there is a clause that allows the organization to change the Terms of Use or Service whenever and however they want.

- Reduce the number of applications you use. Stick to the must-haves.

- Reconsider the benefits versus risks of social media. And if you must use it, curate your connection list to a small group of direct friends and relatives and limit what you post to the bare minimum. Remember that your kids' photos and videos become property of the social media platform. Skip the personality games.

- Delete any application from your mobile device or laptop as soon as you stop using it.

- Don't allow apps on your phone to track your data.

  - This can be a default setting on your mobile phone if you have an Apple device. In April 2021, Apple shipped version 14.5 of its iOS operating system, which introduced a technology called App Tracking Transparency (ATT) that requires apps to get affirmative consent before they can track users by their Identifier for Advertisers (IDFA) or any other identifier.

    - Fun fact: Apple's introduction of ATT had a swift and profound impact on the advertising market. Less than a year later, Facebook disclosed that the iPhone privacy feature would decrease the company's 2022 revenues by about $10 billion.

  - Android users can delete their ad ID permanently, by opening the Settings app and navigating to Privacy ➤ Ads. Tap "Delete advertising ID," then tap it again on the next page to confirm.

- Turn off Location Services if it is not turned off by default, which is a standard implemented on Apple mobile devices.

- Consider a browser with stronger privacy settings such as DuckDuckGo.

- Reject all cookies when visiting websites.

- Delete browser and search history.

- Check the privacy settings of the websites and applications you use. Tailor the settings to reduce any exposure.

  - For example, on LinkedIn, you can modify your Data Privacy settings to not use your data for their generative AI improvement purposes. You can also change the settings in the Advertising Data section, so they don't use your data to allow targeted ads.

- Leverage a DNS-based content filtering solution that prevents people, not only children, from accessing known malicious websites or explicit content online. CleanBrowsing is an example thereof and has additional security and privacy functionalities as well.

- Question the use of transcribing or recording functions used on video calls. Where and for how long is the data kept? If you don't see the value, deny it.

- Review your local state privacy laws. Know your rights and how to file a report or join a class action against an organization who is violating your privacy rights.

- When you get a breach notification letter offering to monitor for identity theft, consider using it provided you don't have to share more sensitive information. But first ensure the actual breach occurred and the letter is legit by calling a contact you know from the breached organization.

- Keep an eye out for solutions to delete your data collected across the World Wide Web. You should be able to permanently delete your account and associated data or restrict how long data can be retained.

  - There is a solution called DeleteMe.com, a service that facilitates its users in deleting their presence on other sites. It also provides information on privacy laws in multiple countries to better educate users on their rights in relation to data privacy.

  - If you need a serious intervention, Delaware-based Atlas Data Privacy Corp. helps its users remove their personal information from the clutches of consumer data brokers and from people-search services online. They have been supporting many class action suits. I have a feeling there will be many more organizations like them.

Summary

Your identity, personal information, and access to other people and organizations are some ways bad actors want to make money. Identity theft will leave you with bad credit and financial ruin. Extortion, ransomware, and ever-changing tactics are increasing in volume and impact. Your financial strength and independence is weakened if you let them take advantage of you.

Data brokers and the monetization of your data as well as the influence campaigns on various media platforms are the formula used to affect our collective behavior. From local to national elections and the polarization resulting in unrest and increased violence could be swayed by one or other masterminds.

Knowing that you must take control of your digital persona, consider the following recommendations:

- Take control of your digital identity and data by protecting it with strong passwords saved in password managers and adding multifactor authentication. Adopt passkeys when possible.

- Keep your technology and underlying software updated.

- Freeze your credit! That is the only way to protect your identity and financial credit worthiness.

- Limit the use of applications to those that are trusted and necessary.

- Limit your adoption of social platforms, and control who has access to what data. Know and exercise your privacy rights.

- Report any and all scams and hacks so the local and federal law enforcement agencies can protect your neighbors, friends, and the greater good.

- As a general rule of thumb, operate with a Zero Trust mindset.

CHAPTER 7

Plan of Action for Educators

Elementary and Secondary Education

Teaching students not only how to use technology but also how to navigate it securely is essential for building a talent pool ready to thrive in a tech-driven world. Let's add a few tools to your curriculum that can expand the horizon for your students and also provide a fundamental knowledge of security and privacy before they dive into cyberspace and join the workforce. Kids love to play games, and cybersecurity can be taught through play and puzzles. It can be learned through teamwork and hands-on collaboration.

A few ideas to keep cybersecurity fun:

- Card games
- Capture the Flag (CTF) games
- Spot the Phish
- Activity books with word puzzles
- Books on cybersecurity careers
- Fiction books and movies

© Cathy Olieslaeger 2025
C. Olieslaeger, *Cybersecurity for Everyone*, Apress Pocket Guides,
https://doi.org/10.1007/979-8-8688-1408-2_7

In addition, have a cybersecurity and privacy day hosted by your local Cyber Hero Squad. Invite cybersecurity professionals to share their story: How did they end up in cybersecurity, what did they want to be growing up, why do they like their job, etc.? *Start with their why.*

Schools need to bring cyber hygiene into their curriculum as soon as computers and Internet-based applications are introduced in the classroom. This should be nonnegotiable, period. Teach the kids about password managers, unique long passphrases, multifactor authentication, and the dangers of social media and online forums.

Set strong rules, communicate them clearly, and enforce them with policies that can be implemented on school computers or firewalls by school system administrators. Ideally, the school's system administrator would create an "allow" list of applications that are safe to be downloaded on the computer and block everything else. This prevents students from downloading applications they shouldn't and prevents malware from being downloaded.

What I learned from hosting cybersecurity day at a Tweens and Technology summer camp and from participating in career days at middle and high schools is that you cannot underestimate these young minds. They are smart! No matter their background and how they perform on tests, keep believing in them, keep cheering for them, and keep introducing new ways to learn cybersecurity. They need to know that you believe in them, and they will believe you. Their potential is endless as long as you are enabling and supporting their growth. *Start with their why.*

> *Education is the most powerful weapon which you can use to change the world.*
>
> —Nelson Mandela

Resources:

- Minimize exposure to cyberattacks and build secure and resilient K-12 cyber systems

  - https://www.schoolsafety.gov/cybersecurity

- A Glossary of Common Cybersecurity Words and Phrases, NICCS

  - https://niccs.cisa.gov/cybersecurity-career-resources/vocabulary

- Podcast: Journey into Cybersecurity (YouTube and any podcast platform)

  - Start with why: https://youtu.be/_pZzMiXO5yQ

  - Words of Wisdom: https://youtu.be/GOZJTsajeKk

- Cybersecurity card games created by CIAS UTSA

  - https://www.youtube.com/@ciasutsa587

  - First game, How to Play Cyber Threat Guardian: https://www.youtube.com/watch?v=KiuhZfVvuko

  - Second game, How to Play Cyber Threat Protector: https://www.youtube.com/watch?v=CkD--gdkYgo

  - Third game to play at home, How to Play Cyber Threat Defender: https://www.youtube.com/watch?v=WJ76DydwejI

- Videos for kids: "We can secure our world!"

  - How to make strong passwords

    https://youtu.be/XXrbut5xRbE?si=udPlbF YTfvUE4S4V

- How to turn on MFA

  `https://youtu.be/QWwaidg3AtY?si=MDdKoT-7X8oblzro`

- How to avoid phishing

  `https://youtu.be/sgOkQYvTlnc?si=rYOQnc1Lzl8SJbGl`

- How to update software

  `https://youtu.be/zCcX6aSXcLI?si=gQd9dL71hEJdDnfE`

- Video on online privacy for kids

  - `https://youtu.be/yiKeLOKc1tw?si=FGojOIqWiyn9wiVV`

- Video for teens on healthy relationships

  - `https://youtu.be/ldjZCvqhNWw`

- Videos and quizzes on Khan Academy on cybersecurity

  - `https://www.khanacademy.org/partner-content/nova/nova-labs-topic/cyber/v/cybersecurity-101`

- Book: Cybersecurity for Teens, an Activity Book, Dfour Press

- Book: Cybersecurity for Teens: Learn the Terms, Daniel Amadi

- Book: See Yourself in Cybersecurity, Zinet Kemal

- Online CTF: `https://hackchallengesforkids.com/`

- TryHackMe CTF: `https://tryhackme.com/`

- Phishing Quiz: `https://www.sonicwall.com/phishing-iq-test/`

There are organizations such as NICE and Cyber.Org that support teachers in their education and adoption of cybersecurity best practices. Follow them, leverage their resources, and consider attending the annual K-12 cybersecurity conference for educators. A more comprehensive list which is maintained on The Triangle Net's website is provided below:

- **The Triangle Net**: K-12 Teacher Resources

    - `https://www.thetrianglenet.com/high-school-cyber-program/`

- **CyberStart America** is the most enjoyable way to discover your talent, advance your skills, and win scholarships in cybersecurity! Free access to immersive cybersecurity games developed for high school students.

    - `https://www.nationalcyberscholarship.org/programs/cyberstartamerica`

    - `https://www.nationalcyberscholarship.org/`

- **K12 Resources for Cybersecurity Education at Home**: Developed by like-minded individuals interested in sharing resources for students, parents, and educators to promote cybersecurity content. Resources curated by the NICE K12 Community of Interest.

    - `https://nicek12athome.weebly.com/`

- **K12 Cybersecurity Education Community of Interest**: This Community of Interest is a forum for K-12 teachers, school administrators, local and state education agencies, nonprofit organizations, federal agencies, institutions of higher education, and others who are interested in sharing and learning how to grow and sustain diverse students pursuing cybersecurity careers through learning experiences, exposure to career opportunities, and teacher professional development.

- `https://www.nist.gov/itl/applied-cybersecurity/nice/community/community-coordinating-council/k12-cybersecurity-education`

- **NICE Cybersecurity Career Awareness Week in October**: Join us in promoting awareness and exploration of cybersecurity careers by hosting an event, participating in an event near you, or engaging students with cybersecurity content!

  - `https://www.nist.gov/itl/applied-cybersecurity/nice/events/cybersecurity-career-week`

- **Free CIAS Card Games**: The UTSA Center for Infrastructure Assurance & Security (CIAS) is committed to creating a culture of cybersecurity through a comprehensive K-12 Cybersecurity Program. The CIAS conducts research into effective ways to introduce students to cybersecurity principles through educational gaming. The program targets four demographics: elementary school, middle school, high school, and colleges/universities. The card game is free to educators!

  - `https://cias.utsa.edu/k-12/`

- **The Last Mile Education Fund**: In addition to the scholarships promoted on our website, consider this educational funding approach meant to empower more students ensuring greater equality and inclusion in STEM education.

    - https://www.lastmile-ed.org/

- **NCWIT Resources for Educators**: NCWIT is a nonprofit community that convenes, equips, and unites change leader organizations to increase the meaningful participation of all women – at the intersections of race, ethnicity, class, age, sexual orientation, and disability status – in the influential field of computing, particularly in terms of innovation and development.

    - https://ncwit.org/k-12/

- **CYBER.ORG Cyber Safety Videos**: CYBER.ORG and the Cybersecurity and Infrastructure Security Agency (CISA) partnered to produce these Cyber Safety Videos. They highlight some common potential threats you're likely to face online and what you can do to make sure you stay safe!

    - https://cyber.org/cybersafety

- **NCyTE Center Cybersecurity Curriculum**: Free cybersecurity curriculum, lessons, and modules designed to help students learn the concepts and skills that employers are seeking. Teachers and cybersecurity experts designed many to align with various portions of curricular frameworks. These teaching resources are intended to be facilitated by an instructor over time.

    - https://www.ncyte.net/faculty/cybersecurity-curriculum

- **NICCS Education and Training Catalog**: The NICCS Education and Training Catalog is a central location where cybersecurity professionals across the nation can find over 6,000 cybersecurity-related courses. Anyone can use the interactive map and filters to search for courses offered in their local area so they can add to their skill set, increase their level of expertise, earn a certification, or even transition into a new career. All of the courses are aligned to the specialty areas of The Workforce Framework for Cybersecurity (NICE Framework).

  - `https://niccs.cisa.gov/education-training/catalog`

- **GenCyber**: The GenCyber program provides summer cybersecurity camp experiences for students and teachers at the K-12 level. The GenCyber program is financially supported by the National Science Foundation and other federal partners on an annual basis.

  - `https://public.cyber.mil/gencyber/`

- **High School Cybersecurity Workshop**: They offer a full curriculum package including student and teacher editions of the lecture notes as well as virtual machine images for running all of their labs. These resources are available for free under a Creative Commons license. The High School Cybersecurity workshop only provides these to educators or to other individuals interested in running a program similar to the one we offer.

  - `https://www.hscybersecurity.org/teachers`

- **CyberPatriot** is the National Youth Cyber Education Program created by the Air Force Association to inspire K-12 students toward careers in cybersecurity or other science, technology, engineering, and mathematics (STEM) disciplines critical to our nation's future. At the core of the program is the National Youth Cyber Defense Competition, the nation's largest cyber defense competition that puts high school and middle school students in charge of securing virtual networks. Other programs include AFA CyberCamps, an elementary school cyber education initiative, a children's literature series.

  - https://www.uscyberpatriot.org/

  - https://www.youtube.com/user/CyberPatriotAFA/videos

- **Microsoft High School Program**: Microsoft offers a variety of resources to help students learn how to code, get internships, and prepare for a career in tech.

  - https://careers.microsoft.com/v2/global/en/discoveryprogram

- **Microsoft for Educators**

  - https://learn.microsoft.com/en-us/training/educator-center/

Higher Education

What skills are needed in cybersecurity? Is it only...

- Vulnerability scanning and patching

- Firewall rule management

- Writing scripts and commands on workstations

- Reading event logs

- Monitoring network traffic

- System administration, etc.

No, we need durable skills in cybersecurity, including

- Adaptability

- Communication

- Compassion and empathy

- Creativity

- Critical thinking

- Cross-functional collaboration

- Curiosity (and no fear of making mistakes)

- Leadership

- Governance

- People management

- Problem-solving

- Risk management

Cybersecurity has many domains, and you cannot limit the learning opportunities to the engineering or architecture of the apparatus. To succeed in cybersecurity, people will need to understand the importance of a cybersecurity-aware culture and executive buy-in, i.e., the people aspect.

On my podcast, **Adrianne George**, an HR Strategist and Advisor, recommended that schools need to stop siloing the different domains. There should be cross-pollination of knowledge across the various domains being taught in higher education. Being able to look at the bigger picture, connect the dots, and adapt to changing circumstances are skills needed in leadership and technology alike. In organizations, job rotation is highly recommended. So you should find ways to expose people to topics that will matter in their career.

Antonio Chousa who had recently graduated with a BS in Cybersecurity mentioned he would have loved to see a class that connects cybersecurity to the business aspects. If you are only educating people to be a cog in a wheel, they may never have the motivation to go all the way. If they see how their work fits in the grand scheme of things and why it matters to implement cybersecurity within products, software, processes, or business administration, you will have a more engaged and productive student.

To that end, recruit and educate students with a purpose in mind. *Start with why!* Show them how cybercrime is harming our healthcare systems, eroding democracy, affecting the elderly, hurting teenagers, and causing real physical and financial harm to people of all walks of life. Show them the trends and annual stats. Tell them we need people in many different roles who understand the importance of cybersecurity, from leadership to those developing new applications and technology and everyone in between.

Every student has their own unique strengths. When you bring a diverse group of students together, combine their strengths to collaborate on a project; that's when the magic happens. Teach them how to collaborate, think outside the box, consult diverse opinions, challenge groupthink, and ultimately how to make decisions based on business impact, operational resilience, and the safety of people first and foremost.

CHAPTER 8

Plan of Action for Students

Where to Start?

So you wish to pursue a cybersecurity education? Awesome! The good news is that you have choices. The bad news is that it is not easy to make a choice. Here are some questions I ask my mentees when we first meet. Let these simmer in your head for a while before you make any big moves.

Where did you come from?

- What were you like as a kid?

- Were you into computers, gaming, building legos, breaking things?

- Were you artistic, a creative thinker?

- Did you like to solve puzzles?

- Do you like to help people?

- What classes did you enjoy in high school?

- What kind of student jobs have you pursued? What could you build on?

© Cathy Olieslaeger 2025
C. Olieslaeger, *Cybersecurity for Everyone*, Apress Pocket Guides,
https://doi.org/10.1007/979-8-8688-1408-2_8

- Who were your cheerleaders? Why did they believe in you?

- Who were your role models? What did you like about them?

Where are you going?

- What attracts you to cybersecurity?

- Who are your role models?

- Do you like to collaborate or prefer to work alone?

- Do you like a structured and predictable schedule? Or do you like change and don't mind a challenge that could keep you up all night?

- Do you see yourself in a leadership position?

- How do you like to learn?

- What kind of organization would you prefer to work for? Small or big, startup or mature, public or private?

- Depending on your age and life stage you're in, could you afford to travel a lot for work?

- Do you need flexibility to care for children, parents, or others?

- Would you prefer working remotely, in an office, or a hybrid arrangement?

What is your why?

- Do you know your values? What are they?

- How would you know whether an organization has the same values as you? Do you know what to look for?

- How do you see yourself helping others?

- Consider becoming a mentor. Can you think of anyone who you can help right now?

- Do you like to teach?

- How can you share your lessons learned?

What are your next steps?

- What skills do you want to develop: social engineering, open source intelligence (OSINT), threat intelligence, entrepreneurship, business administration, security operations, sales engineering, secure software development, blue team or red team testing, GRC, teaching...

- Who would be a good mentor or role model? Engage them.

- What organizations specialize in your areas of interest? Follow them.

- What types of jobs or skills are in high demand?

- What resources do you need to take that next best step?

To get a feel of the market demand for cybersecurity talent, you can consult the CyberSeek Interactive Map which allows you to determine how many cybersecurity job openings exist in your state and what type of jobs are available. In another tab, the CyberSeek Career Pathway shows you a few types of entry roles and how you can move up on the cybersecurity ladder. It shows details around the skills, education, and salary expectations for each role. Pretty cool!

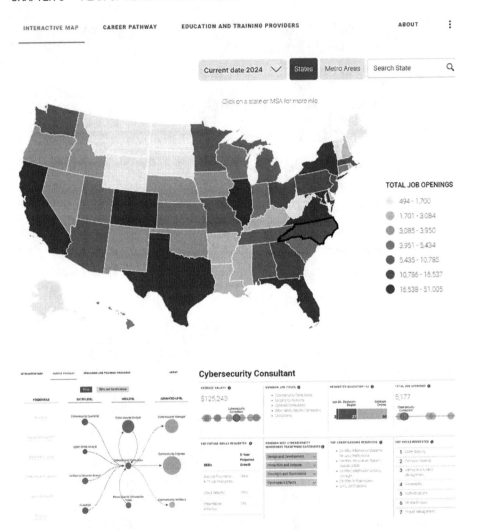

As you go through the process of determining which first step to take, what type of education to invest in, and what area to specialize in, remember to consult the pros.

> *Life's most persistent and urgent question is, 'What are you doing for others?'*
>
> —Dr. Martin Luther King Jr.

Resources:

- CyberSeek Interactive Map

    - `https://www.cyberseek.org/heatmap.html`

- CyberSeek Career Pathway

    - `https://www.cyberseek.org/pathway.html`

Find Your Tribe

Join a local cybersecurity association (ISSA, ISACA, (ISC)2, OWASP, WiCyS, CSA, etc.) and attend their networking events and conferences. Identify a few people who could be good role models or mentors as you journey into cybersecurity. They would be more than honored to help you, believe me. All you have to do is ask. How? Start with "I need help as I start my cybersecurity education or career. It's a bit daunting and overwhelming. Could you spare some time to share your ideas with me and guide me in the right direction?" Easy.

Resources:

- ISSA

    - `https://www.issa.org/`

- ISACA

    - `https://www.isaca.org/`

- (ISC)2

    - `https://www.isc2.org/`

- OWASP

    - `https://owasp.org/`

- WiCyS

  - https://www.wicys.org/

- CSA

  - https://cloudsecurityalliance.org/

- Find your Tribe, The Triangle Net website

  - https://www.thetrianglenet.com/join-us/

Mentorship Versus Sponsorship

Nobody in cybersecurity ever claims they reached the top all by themselves. We are all standing on the shoulders of people who believed in us, took a chance on us, invested in us, and supported us on our journey. There is no stronger community than the cybersecurity community. During any point in your career, there is tremendous value in nurturing a relationship with a mentor and ultimately becoming one as well. Their experience, insights, and network can benefit you. Lots of organizations offer mentorship programs where you can apply to receive mentorship. It doesn't hurt however to identify thought leaders in the cybersecurity domain and subdomain you are interested in and reach out via LinkedIn or in person if you have the opportunity. Just you taking that initiative will catch their attention.

Once you have the blessing of a mentor, make sure you take every piece of advice to heart. If they give you homework, do it and follow up. Too often, mentors complain that their mentees just want the advice, the introduction, and then the job without putting in the work. You have to earn their trust before you can earn their vote. Earn it.

There are mentors and then there are sponsors. Sponsors are the people who will recommend you even when you're not in the room. They put their weight behind their endorsement of you. They are promoters of you. Treasure these folks as they are priceless.

After everything is said and done, turn around and look behind you. Who could you mentor? Who would you go to bat for? Pay it forward.

Stay away from the negative people. They have a problem for every solution.

—Albert Einstein

Resources:

- The Triangle Net, Mentorships
    - `https://www.thetrianglenet.com/mentorships-internships-jobs/`
- ISSA AIM (Apprenticeships, Internships, and Mentorships)
    - `https://www.issa.org/what-is-aim-program/`
- Book: Pathfinders, Navigating Your Career Map with a Personal Board of Advisors, Pete Schramm
    - `https://golattitude.com/pathfinders-book/`

Knowledge Is Power
Curate Your Feed

In addition to joining an association and networking events, start following cybersecurity professionals, teachers, students, and organizations on social media. I prefer LinkedIn, which is to me more professional and less noisy than others. But who knows what social media and digital networking will look like five years from now? You want to follow trends, stay up to date on threats and technology, and understand regulations and shifts in standards. Change will be constant; you have to keep up. By keeping an eye on trends and new developments, you could develop an edge and become a subject matter expert in an innovative domain. Just keep your mind, eyes, and ears open. Think critically when consuming anything on social media, so curate your feed with only trustworthy sources.

Free Content to Get the Lay of the Land

Whether it's online or in person, there are many ways to gain knowledge for free! There are lots of podcasts and webinars you could listen to. The podcasts that I recommend include *Darknet Diaries* and *The CyberWire*. They give you great content on all kinds of cybersecurity-related topics and are constantly sharing the latest and greatest innovations and threats. I recommend you check out the *Journey into Cybersecurity* podcast to determine which type of role you see yourself filling. Each guest plays a different role in different types of organizations, so they make it easy for you to see yourself in their shoes. Some conferences are recorded and shared on the organization's website and YouTube channel. Be resourceful and keep digging.

Resources:

- Podcasts

    - Darknet Diaries

        `https://darknetdiaries.com/`

    - The CyberWire

        `https://thecyberwire.com/`

    - Journey into Cybersecurity

        `https://www.thetrianglenet.com/journey-into-cybersecurity/`

- The Triangle Net resources

    - `https://www.thetrianglenet.com/resources/`

- Raleigh InfoSeCon Recordings of Presentations

    - `https://www.triangleinfosecon.com/`

    - `https://www.youtube.com/@RaleighISSA`

Educational Paths

When it comes to your educational options, there are a few. The way you answer some of the questions above may help you determine which options are a better fit and which options you should put on the backburner. There is a variety when it comes to college or university degrees: associate's, bachelor's, master's, and beyond. If you are pivoting your career path, there are alternative ways to learn the fundamentals and expertise in a subdomain, without having to quit your day job.

Check out CompTIA's Security+, (ISC)2 Cybersecurity Certification, or Google's Cybersecurity Certificate to learn the fundamentals. Microsoft and AWS also provide free training. Learning is something that is very unique to your own preferences, so figure out how you like to learn. You definitely should get the book, leverage practice tests, and watch some of the free YouTube channels (e.g., Professor Messer) on them. Create flash cards as a means to help you memorize the acronyms.

If your budget is tight, check with local security associations as they often donate books and even your local library. Ask your employer if they have a tuition reimbursement program. Leverage scholarships from technology organizations and cybersecurity associations. The possibilities to make your education affordable are endless!

The Security+ certification is often a minimum requirement for any entry-level cybersecurity job; consider it as a way to get your foot in the door. Based on the types of job roles you wish to pursue, check out job postings to see what the minimum requirements are as well as the technology that is most commonly used in these roles. You can add a specialization in a toolset that complements your theoretical knowledge. This can include

- Cloud Security Posture Management (CSPM) solutions such as Amazon, Microsoft, Google, Wiz, etc.

- SIEM and incident detection and response solutions such as Splunk, CrowdStrike, Sentinel, Sumo Logic, etc.

- Network and infrastructure security tools such as vulnerability scanning, network traffic monitoring, or firewall management such as Qualys, Nessus, WireShark, Palo Alto, etc. This area is expanding into attack surface management (ASM) and continuous threat exposure management (CTEM) where the focus is on identifying, classifying and protecting assets on an ongoing, risk-based and automated basis.

Hands-on experiences such as CTFs and labs will add a boost to your profile.

Luck is where preparation meets opportunity.

—Randy Pausch

Resources:

- The Triangle Net Educational Resources

  - `https://www.thetrianglenet.com/learning/`
- CompTIA Security+

  - `https://www.comptia.org/certifications/security`

- (ISC)2 Certified in Cybersecurity

  - `https://www.isc2.org/certifications/cc`

- Google Cybersecurity Certificate

  - `https://grow.google/certificates/cybersecurity/`

- Professor Messer YouTube

  - `https://www.youtube.com/professormesser`

- Microsoft security training

  - `https://learn.microsoft.com/en-us/training/`

- Microsoft Zero Trust description

  - `https://www.microsoft.com/en-us/videoplayer/embed/RE4J3ms?postJsllMsg=true`

- Cyber degrees

  - `https://www.cyberdegrees.org/`

Cybersecurity Governance, Risk, and Compliance

I strongly believe that Governance, Risk, and Compliance (GRC) is a great point of entry into cybersecurity. You shouldn't have to go through multiple coding courses that you absolutely are not interested in and that are just eroding your enthusiasm for the domain. Not everyone should become a security analyst in a Security Operations Center (SOC) or a penetration tester. There are many alternatives to the technical path into cybersecurity. Understanding some of the most widely adopted cybersecurity and privacy frameworks, regulations, and standards is a great start. It builds a picture and structure in your mind and can help you figure out what else you wish to learn.

The *NIST Cybersecurity Framework* (CSF) or the *Center for Internet Security (CIS) Top 18* are a great start. These frameworks are available online; read them. In addition, widely adopted standards include *NIST SP 800-53* and *ISO/IEC 27001 and 27002* (more prevalent in Europe and Asia). Some types of data have specific security requirements either imposed by a regulator or the industry itself. The healthcare vertical has the HIPAA Security, Privacy, and Breach Notification Rules, while any merchant wanting to take credit card payments has to abide by the Payment Card Industry (PCI) Data Security Standard (DSS) no matter where they are in the world.

In addition, privacy regulations are growing in numbers. Europe's *GDPR* and California's *CCPA* are some of the higher standards around privacy which focus more on the protection of citizens' personal identifiable information (PII) and data confidentiality. Because every US state has some sort of local privacy and breach notification law, the common denominator often becomes the highest standard of them all.

Finally, risk management is becoming more central to cybersecurity frameworks and the programs organizations have to implement. Both NIST, and ISO have cybersecurity risk management frameworks that help identify and qualify cybersecurity risks. FAIR as well as CIS RAM are complementary frameworks that quantify cybersecurity risks. What's the difference?

- **Qualitative models** use metrics to determine the likelihood and impact of a risk that are either numbers (1–5) or words (very low to very high); they may add some colors to get the point across (i.e., green is good, red is bad).

- **Quantitative models** provide financial metrics to quantify the risk. They boil it all down to the way a security incident could affect the financial bottom line of the organization. That may get you the attention and

executive buy-in you need to invest in risk mitigation
strategies that strengthen the organization's security
posture and long-term resilience.

Keep an eye on this space as automation, data science, and soon
enough AI will help make these quantifications more real time, relevant,
and accurate. Knowing how to pull all this data into a business intelligence
(BI) tool like Tableau, PowerBI, or others and make the data easy to digest
is a critical communication tool in this process. Make sure you always
tailor the presentation to the audience and keep it simple.

If cybersecurity governance and leadership is your goal, the *ISACA
CISM* and *(ISC)2 CISSP* are the most commonly required certifications
to make it to the top. They are not created equal though. Like any
cybersecurity certification, the curriculum does get updated on a regular
basis to keep up with the ever-changing technology, regulatory, and threat
landscape. To receive the actual certification, you also have to meet criteria
beyond passing an exam including a minimum number of years of work
experience in cybersecurity and other types of education.

The amount of GRC-focused certifications has grown tremendously.
There are additional programs available to support future Chief
Information Security Officers (CISOs) in their pursuit of the top cyber
job. Having a business administration degree and business leadership
experience is a big plus to complement the cybersecurity certs and degrees
you have accumulated. The greater your perspective on cyber risk and
business, the greater value you bring to the table.

The ISACA CISM includes the following domains:

- Information Security Governance

- Information Risk Management

- Information Security Program Development and
  Management

- Information Security Incident Management

The (ISC)2 CISSP includes a broader set of domains:

- Security and Risk Management

- Asset Security

- Security Architecture and Engineering

- Communication and Network Security

- Identity and Access Management

- Security Testing and Assessment

- Security Operations

- Software Development Security

Resources:

- NIST CSF

  - https://nvlpubs.nist.gov/nistpubs/CSWP/NIST.CSWP.29.pdf

- CIS Top 18

  - https://www.cisecurity.org/controls/cis-controls-list

- HIPAA regulations

  - https://www.hhs.gov/hipaa/for-professionals/index.html

- PCI DSS

  - https://www.pcisecuritystandards.org/

- EU GDPR

  - https://gdpr.eu/what-is-gdpr/

- California's Consumer Privacy Act (CCPA)

    - `https://oag.ca.gov/privacy/ccpa`

- ISACA CISM

    - `https://www.isaca.org/credentialing/cism`

- (ISC)2 certifications incl. CISSP

    - `https://www.isc2.org/Certifications`

- GRC Learning Resources

    - `https://www.thetrianglenet.com/grc/`

- Simply Cyber, The Definitive GRC Analyst Program

    - `https://academy.simplycyber.io/p/the-definitive-grc-analyst-program`

What's Your Next Best Step?

The learning never ends. Always ponder the question: What is my next best step? There are some tools and graphical displays of how your journey into cybersecurity may meander different subdomains. By combining knowledge and experience in a few of them, you gain greater perspective and a unique edge. A few examples...

The *National Initiative for Cybersecurity Careers and Studies (NICCS)* has an interactive online Cyber Career Pathways Tool that allows you to connect the dots within a subdomain and beyond. As the diagram shows, cybersecurity stretches into many cross-functional domains such as legal, law enforcement, lifecycle, talent, and strategic management. Cybersecurity is a place where you can start or end your career. Either way, cybersecurity knowledge will be instrumental in any role you will ever play!

The tool allows you to see what knowledge and skills are needed with each role, all 52 of them. Not all are super technical. I am pretty confident that you can find a bubble in this tool that speaks to you and gives you some guidance on what to do next.

About the Cyber Workforce Communities Venn Diagram

The Cyber Workforce encompasses the skills required to **build**, **secure**, **operate**, **defend** and **protect** technology, data, and resources; **conduct** related **intelligence** activities; enable **future operations**; and **project power** in or through cyberspace. It is comprised of the following skill communities: **IT, Cybersecurity, Cyber Effects, Intel (Cyber), and Cross Functional.** The skill communities are color coded to match the work role galaxy.

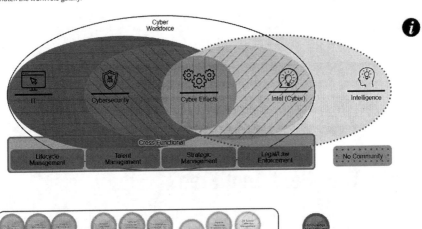

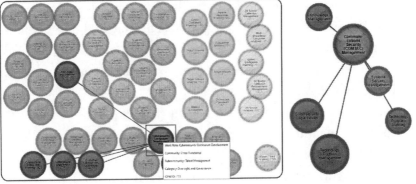

SANS published a poster on their website with the 20 coolest careers in cybersecurity. They include

1. Threat Hunter (Threat/Warning Analyst)

2. Red Teamer (Adversary Emulation Specialist)

3. Digital Forensics Analyst

4. Purple Teamer

5. Malware Analyst

6. Chief Information Security Officer (CISO) (Executive Cyber Leadership)

7. Blue Teamer – All-Around Defender (Cyber Defense Analyst)

8. Security Architect (NICE) and Engineer

9. Cyber Defense Incident Responder/Law Enforcement Counterintelligence Forensics Analyst

10. Cybersecurity Analyst/Engineer (Systems Security Analyst)

11. OSINT Investigator/Analyst

12. Technical Director (Information Systems Security Manager)

13. Cloud Security Analyst

14. Intrusion Detection/SOC Analyst (Cyber Defense Analyst)

15. Security Awareness Officer (Security Awareness and Communications Manager)

16. Vulnerability Researcher and Exploit Developer (Vulnerability Assessment Analyst)

17. Application Pen Tester (Secure Software Accessor)

18. ICS/OT Security Assessment Consultant (ICS/SCADA Security Engineer)

19. DevSecOps Engineer

20. Media Exploitation Analyst (Cyber Crime Investigator)

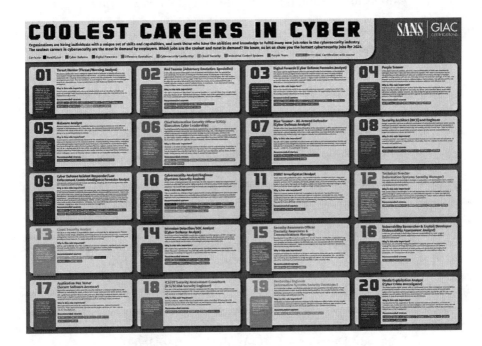

Resources:

- NICCS Cyber Career Pathways Tool

    - `https://niccs.cisa.gov/workforce-development/cyber-career-pathways-tool?selected-role=OG-WRL-009`

- SANS 20 Coolest Careers in Cyber

  - `https://www.sans.org/cybersecurity-careers/20-coolest-cyber-security-careers/`

Build and Leverage Your Durable Skills

There are many other ways to participate in the business and purpose of cybersecurity. Here is a listing of cyber enabling jobs that are worth investigating depending on your strengths, skills, experience, and interests.

- Law Enforcement Counterintelligence Forensics Analyst

- Cyber Crime Investigator

- Cyber Instructional Curriculum Developer

- Cyber Instructor

- Cyber Legal Advisor

- Privacy Officer, Privacy Compliance Officer

- Cyber Workforce Developer and Manager

- Cyber Policy Strategy Planner

- Program Manager

- IT Project Manager

- Product Support Manager

- IT Investment Portfolio Manager

- IT Program Auditor

- Executive Cyber Leadership

And if those are not compelling enough, consider a Sales or Marketing role in an organization, big or small, where your durable skills will be augmented by the knowledge of the product or service you will be bringing to the world. It is worth noting that these jobs can be very lucrative if you put your heart and grit in it. If you like to socialize, collaborate, and help people, you may be meant to be in Sales.

There are many types of roles within a Sales and Marketing organization. They include Product Marketing, Event Management, Multichannel Communications, Market Intelligence, Sales Operations, Business Development, (Technical) Account Management, Sales Engineering, Customer Success Management, Partner Program Management, and Service Delivery.

All these people need leadership that inspires, supports, empowers, and rewards them every step of the way. Here are some durable skills, also called transferable skills, that can benefit you in this role:

- **Leadership**: Inspire people to take action and deliver positive results. Build trust by being vulnerable and authentic.

- **Character**: Lead by example and with integrity. Stay true to yourself and your values.

- **Collaboration**: Collaborate with your colleagues by giving them a seat at the table and hearing their voice.

- **Communication**: Share information with your audience in a way that aligns with their interests and relate it to what matters to them.

- **Creativity**: Keep challenging the status quo, look at a problem from different angles, and think outside the box.

- **Critical thinking**: Develop informed ideas and effective solutions. Ask "what if" questions.

- **Metacognition**: Self-understanding and personal management. Do you understand the effect your actions and words have on people?

- **Mindfulness**: Interpersonal and self-awareness.

- **Growth Mindset**: Be willing to be challenged and keep learning from your experiences and other perspectives.

- **Fortitude**: Constitution and inspiration. You are not defined by your circumstances, but by how you handle them.

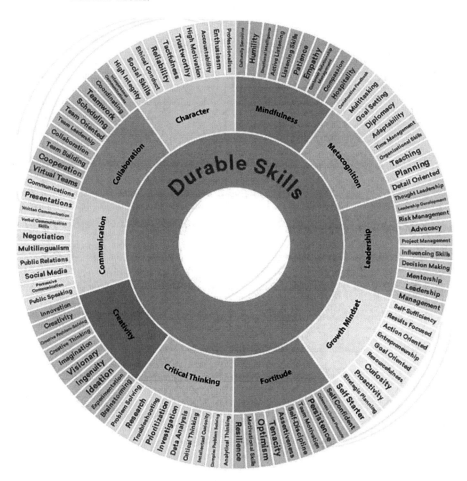

It is important to note that your ability to communicate and collaborate with people across an organization is absolutely critical. Being mindful of your audience and the language they use in their day-to-day life is part of this skillset. Business leaders don't speak cyber, so don't use acronyms or metrics that don't mean anything to them. Make the message relevant to them so it allows them to make business decisions and take action that benefit everyone. People and organizations can only be successful and resilient if everyone is equally invested in the shared purpose of protecting the organization you work for and the greater good. Never lose sight of the importance of your role in the grand scheme of things. You matter; use your voice to make a real difference.

Speak the truth even if your voice shakes.

—Maggie Kuhn

Unlike its IQ sibling and whatever is believed about IQ, emotional intelligence or EQ is something that you can build and develop over time. Your brain is a fascinating part of your body that you can keep nurturing and developing at any age. Emotional intelligence is a critical component in your personal and professional development you must invest in.

Daniel Goleman is the author who brought the study of emotional intelligence to the masses. His books *Emotional Intelligence: Why It Can Matter More Than IQ* and *Focus* will help you understand the power you have within and how to unleash it. Emotional intelligence can be broken down into four domains:

- Self-awareness
- Self-management
- Social awareness which includes empathy
- Relationship management which includes social skills

As our personal and professional lives are more and more dominated by technology, especially in remote work environments, being able to demonstrate your authenticity, build trust, and collaborate closely with people in a way where everyone has a voice and is heard, these skills will matter more and more.

On the topic of trust, it is absolutely critical to recognize that trust is THE product in the cybersecurity domain. This is your product as a person and the product your organization sells. People hire people they trust. People buy from people they trust. Loyalty is a by-product of trust. If you cannot build relationships on the basis of trust, you will have a problem sustaining a successful career in any domain. But in cybersecurity, where we are protecting the most critical elements of our society and sustaining a business, trust is everything!

So when you show up for a job interview or to a working session or in any other scenario, be yourself, be honest, and be open about the things you don't know. On the flip side, be careful about who you trust. Trust must be earned through action, not words.

Trust is the bedrock of a great team.

—Patrick Lencioni

Resources:

- Pathways, cyber enabling jobs

  - `https://public.cyber.mil/wid/pathways/`

- How to Be an Ethical Hacker in 2025, TCM Security

  - `https://tcm-sec.com/how-to-be-an-ethical-hacker-in-2025/`

- Durable Skills

  - `https://durableskills.org/`

- Video: The 4 domains of emotional intelligence, Daniel Goleman

  - `https://youtu.be/erfgEHHfFkU?si=MYt5Yrrq IlZBb2Ul`

- Book: Emotional Intelligence: Why It Can Matter More than IQ, Daniel Goleman

    - `https://www.goodreads.com/book/show/26329.`
    `Emotional_Intelligence?ref=nav_sb_ss_1_54`

- Book: Focus: The Hidden Driver of Excellence, Daniel Goleman

    - `https://www.goodreads.com/book/`
    `show/17349126-focus?ref=nav_sb_ss_2_20`

- Book: Emotional Intelligence 2.0, Travis Bradberry and Jean Greaves

    - `https://www.goodreads.com/book/show/6486483-`
    `emotional-intelligence-2-0?ref=nav_sb_ss_1_26`

- Book: The Five Dysfunctions of a Team, Patrick Lencioni

    - `https://www.goodreads.com/book/show/21343.`
    `The_Five_Dysfunctions_of_a_Team?ref=nav_`
    `sb_ss_1_31`

- Video: What Is Trust Actually?, Simon Sinek (YouTube)

    - `https://youtu.be/wz1vmOjae2O?si=eYlbOVS3sH6ipDm6`

Experience Matters

Capture the Flag

Find hands-on or in-person learning opportunities. Capture the Flag (CTF) events are available everywhere. You can also find online CTF platforms that can teach you a few tricks and expand your knowledge. CTF competitions are also great collaboration opportunities and ways to meet fellow students and professionals.

The NSA in the United States also has supported cybersecurity camps for students in collaboration with local universities across the country. GenCyber is a great opportunity to get some exposure to the domain, people who work in cybersecurity, and fellow students who pursue the same purpose.

You will make friends and potentially meet your future employer at these events. So bring your A-game and your willingness to make mistakes and learn from them. That is the most important goal of these events: to learn from your mistakes and share your lessons learned. You are not competing with other students or professionals. You are competing with the bad guys; don't forget!

Resources:

- GenCyber: `https://public.cyber.mil/gencyber/camp-catalog/`

- TryHackMe CTF: `https://tryhackme.com/`

- HackTheBox CTF: `https://www.hackthebox.com/hacker/ctf`

- Pico CTF: `https://picoctf.org/`

Internships

Find an internship, full time if your schedule affords it or during summer break. Start looking for an internship the fall before summer; that's right, nine months in advance. Check out

- The Triangle Net Internships

  - `https://www.thetrianglenet.com/mentorships-internships-jobs/`

- Indeed Internships

  - `https://www.indeed.com/jobs?q=cyber+security+internship&l=United+States&vjk=d01743f2aec49887`

- LinkedIn Internships
  - `https://www.internships.com`
- Apprenticeships
  - `https://www.apprenticeship.gov/`
- ISSA AIM (Apprenticeships, Internships, and Mentorships)
  - `https://www.issa.org/what-is-aim-program/`
- CompTIA Apprenticeships
  - `https://www.comptia.org/content/lp/apprenticeships-for-tech`
- Microsoft Student Programs
  - `https://careers.microsoft.com/v2/global/en/programs/students.html`
- Handshake for Students
  - `https://joinhandshake.com/students/`

Ask your school's advisor if they have any business connections where internships are being offered. Oftentimes, schools have partnerships with local employers. If they don't, urge them to build one and offer to help.

Scholarships

Organizations recognize that education can create a financial burden on families and students. Many offer scholarships. Look for them and see if you can strike gold. There are also scholarships to support your participation in cybersecurity conferences. Take advantage of those. And if you can't find one, ask around. You may run into an organization or someone who would love to sponsor you and your continued learning journey.

Resources:

- The Triangle Net Scholarship Listing

    - https://www.thetrianglenet.com/scholarships/

- WiCyS scholarships for girls and women

    - https://www.wicys.org/initiatives/programs/

- (ISC)2 and Center for Cyber Safety and Education

    - https://www.iamcybersafe.org/s/scholarships

- ISSA

    - https://issaef.org/scholarships/apply/

If you don't ask, the answer is always no.

—Nora Roberts

Pay It Forward!

I'm of the strong belief that you get what you give. When you learn something cool, share it! When you reached a major milestone, share how you got there. When you read something interesting, share what you took away from it. If someone helps you, recognize them and pay it forward. Help someone else. Look behind you and see if another kid could use a hand just like you once did. Be a cheerleader. Be a mentor. Be a study buddy. Thank a teacher. Be kind. The world needs you. Give.

You matter! - Neil Degrasse Tyson

For the Ladies

The world has all kinds of opinions about what a woman can and cannot do. If you turn on the television, social media, or streaming apps, there seems to be a consistent message that girls and women are imperfect, incapable, or incompetent. But you and I know better.

Confidence is not something you gain from consuming products marketed to you on the basis of your poor self-image. No makeup or Gucci bag can build you up like you can. Let them try selling you their plastic dreams and superficial perfection. Be critical when you give your time, attention, and money to anyone or anything. What or who is the product? "What's in it for me?" should be the question you ask when consuming anything.

Imposter syndrome is real! We have to thank the capitalistic and biased world we live in for that and all the marketing campaigns that portray women as servants and consumers and not as leaders and creators. Am I worthy? Am I good enough? Am I smart enough? Do I qualify enough for this job? It's society's vicious voice that keeps you from even trying.

You do have a choice though! Do you choose to believe them or do you believe in you? Do you listen to the negative messages or do you listen to your inner voice cheering you on and moving you forward? You absolutely have to invest in yourself in a way that will grow your confidence. Learn more and do more. (Don't spend more!) Over time, one step at a time, your confidence will grow. Use your time and energy very carefully. Only you can decide what you do with it.

Hiring practices remain very subjective. People are hired on the basis of confidence they exude, which is something most men don't lack. They are confident in their abilities, so let's believe them! You will have to challenge the system to hire for competence and not only for confidence. Show them what you've done to get to where you are right now. Show them your plan of action to keep learning and creating more value to the lucky ones who get to work with you. Meritocracy will be the standard that raises girls and women to where they belong: in every position imaginable and more importantly in a position of leadership where they can empower more people deserving of an equal opportunity.

All the adversity in the world is just a test. How badly do you want this? How important is this to you? Why does it matter that you overcome this obstacle? In Randy Pausch's book and presentation titled *The Last Lecture*, he talks about these "brick walls" and how everything is just a test of your will and your power to persevere no matter what life throws at you. Show them what you are made of! No matter how hard things get, don't let the fear of failure make you quit. Quitting is failure; everything else is a life lesson. Keep going!

You will never make it on your own. Yes, invest in yourself, your education, and gaining experiences that enrich your value. But you absolutely must invest in building a network that wants to support you. How? First, identify people who can be your mentor and don't limit yourself to women. There are many men who want to be allies to women and believe in equal opportunity and the unique value women bring to the table. In addition to mentors, find people who will be your sponsor. They are the ones who will recommend you when you're not even in the room. They are more than a cheerleader; they are a promoter. Finally, join organizations supporting women such as Women in CyberSecurity (WiCyS) and be an active participant. Consider volunteering within cybersecurity or STEM associations to demonstrate your commitment and work ethic. Find your tribe and earn their trust. We've got you!

Every girl, no matter where she lives, deserves the opportunity to develop the promise inside of her.

—Michelle Obama

Believe!

Here are my final two cents. Just know that you are standing in front of an endless world of opportunities and possibilities. Your potential has no boundaries. Focus on your next best step based on your awareness of your strengths, your values, and how you wish to make a positive impact on your community. The only person standing between you and your success is you. Believe in yourself and trust that you can make a difference. You got this!

The genius thing that we did was, we didn't give up.

—Jay-Z

CHAPTER 9

Plan of Action for Hiring Managers and HR Leaders

Build a People Strategy

Does your organization have a people strategy? Does it align with the business strategy? Is it funded appropriately? What is the people strategy within your cybersecurity and risk management strategy? As you implement a security or cyber risk management program, how will you rely on resources across the organization? What skills will they need?

If you struggle building a people strategy in general or around cybersecurity in particular, consider hiring an HR strategist and advisor, someone who understands both the cybersecurity and HR aspects and can translate the needs from the cybersecurity group into a people strategy that may include hiring interns, contractors, and new employees or developing training and talent retention programs.

Look at your team and the broader organization as a puzzle. Every person has a unique skill set, background, and perspective. They are not just a static two-page resume. Are you recognizing this, documenting it,

C. Olieslaeger, *Cybersecurity for Everyone*, Apress Pocket Guides, https://doi.org/10.1007/979-8-8688-1408-2_9

and asking employees how they wish to use their strengths beyond their current job? Do they have more potential than meets the eye? Regular "performance" reviews or simple conversations around the person's experience on the job can give you many insights and opportunities to create more value together. Be invested in your people, and they will repay you in spades.

Build a Hiring Strategy

In close collaboration with the HR team and your leadership, build a people strategy and a hiring process that will get you the best results in the short- and long-term run. Be mindful of the bias that may exist in your organization and determine in advance how you will ensure the right person is hired for the job, how you will engage them and invest in their continued growth, and how you will support their career objectives over time.

While you may see yourself in a position of power when going through the recruitment process and beyond, you need to remember that the hiring process is a two-way street. You need to compel the person to work for and with you. When they get smarter and more experienced over time, you have to ensure that they will want to stay. The number one reason why people quit their job is because of their manager. That's you.

While you may want to hire a unicorn who can do it all and knows it all, you must remain realistic in your expectations. Make sure that job descriptions reflect that. Ask yourself two questions: What are the must-have skills that we need out of the gate and what can I teach them on the job? Does a certain degree or amount of experience in years guarantee these skills? If not, why add more barriers to the hiring process than is necessary?

When it comes to hiring cybersecurity talent with a specialization in analytics, a SOC analyst or a technical tester, for instance, you should customize your hiring process to account for the unique candidates who can fill those roles. These technical and more tactical roles can be filled with people whose strengths include pattern detection, an attention to detail, and a strong determination to solve puzzles. Sometimes, these individuals are more introverted, maybe socially awkward, and could be neurodiverse. While they may not perform well during an interview, they would perform very well as an analyst. A Dark Reading article provides "Eight Tips for Hiring and Training Neurodivergent Talent," which are

- Embrace performance-based interviews
- Communicate clear expectations
- Use flexible interview formats
- Develop individualized training plans
- Build a culture of inclusion
- Implement universal design principles
- Regularly check in with employees
- Be open to learning and adapting

In his book *Great People Decisions: Why They Matter So Much, Why They Are So Hard, and How You Can Master Them*, Claudio Fernandez Araoz identifies four core key executive and five second-tier competencies that you should look for when hiring a leader such as a CISO in your organization.

Four core key executive competencies:

- Strong results orientation
- Team leadership
- Collaboration and influence
- Strategic orientation

Five second-tier competencies:

- Commercial orientation

- Change leadership

- Developing organizational capability

- Customer impact

- Market knowledge

If you judge a fish by its ability to climb a tree, it will live its whole life believing that it is stupid.

—Albert Einstein

Build a Retention and Succession Strategy

Human Resource management is not only about hiring people and letting them figure out the rest once they're in the door. When it comes to cybersecurity talent, once they have enough education and work experience, they will have many opportunities thrown at them at all times. Retention in cybersecurity is a challenge today, often caused by stress, burnout, poor leadership, lack of resources, or simply a higher compensation package.

To retain your cybersecurity team, and especially the CISO, you will need to build a program that supports their needs (financial, family, growth, health, etc.). Assume that they may want to try different roles, learn new things, and that they may need to delegate certain responsibilities to other team members over time.

Building a bench to address people leaving or being promoted should also be part of your people strategy. When someone leaves, make sure to have an exit interview to get to the root of their departure. Even though pay is commonly given as the reason, nobody likes to work for a jerk. Maybe it's better to get rid of the jerk than to lose the people who know best how to protect your organization.

You Can't Get What You Don't Give

There is a gap between the educational and professional stages of a young person or a professional looking to pivot into cybersecurity. An organization cannot expect their future hires to have work experience if they do not offer internships or entry-level jobs themselves. Every organization should have internships available, in particular in the technology domains. You cannot expect a person to know how to operate every piece of equipment and software you have. There are hundreds and thousands of technology solutions in IT and cybersecurity. Look for transferable skills, a growth mindset, and a strong work ethic, then teach new hires how you use technology and processes to protect your organization. Give.

Build Bridges

Organizations often complain that young graduates lack certain skills. Boo hoo! Create a cooperative with local schools or join an advisory board at a university or college so you can educate educators on the skills and qualifications you are looking for. You know better what is around the corner than anyone else. Make education your business and become part of the solution to reduce the so-called talent gap. Promote volunteering and offer volunteer time off so you and your team can be invested in your community. Be part of something bigger than yourself or your organization.

Be Visible

Finally, be a role model. Talk to your local middle and high schools, their PTA, or CTE teachers and offer to host a cybersecurity lunch and learn, career day, or teach the kids about privacy and how to be safe online. Ladies, if you want more women in cybersecurity, you will need to show young girls that there is a place for them where you work.

When you share your story, *start with why* you do what you do. Offer your mentorship, offer job shadowing opportunities, create an internship for all the tasks you would love to not do, and watch your impact grow. I promise, you will find fulfillment and joy in doing so. You are meant to be a role model. Start now!

CHAPTER 10

Plan of Action for Business Leaders

Get Your People Strategy Right

To be a resilient organization, you have to get your people strategy right first.

Does the Chief Information Security Officer (CISO) in your organization have a seat at your table? Do they have a voice in business planning meetings? Do you listen to them and provide them with the resources they need to succeed in the execution of their cyber risk management strategy, which is part of your business and ERM strategy?

Does the Chief People Officer participate in your strategic planning, and are they supported in the execution of your people strategy? Is the people strategy part of the cyber risk management strategy? Do you empower them to hire and retain people who can positively impact your security risk posture? Are you involved in eliminating bias from the hiring process?

© Cathy Olieslaeger 2025
C. Olieslaeger, *Cybersecurity for Everyone*, Apress Pocket Guides,
https://doi.org/10.1007/979-8-8688-1408-2_10

Patrick Lencioni has identified "Six Types of Working Genius" or intelligence types which get a team or organization from point A to point B. They are

- **Wonder**: The ability to ask questions and generate ideas that spark curiosity and interest

- **Invention**: The ability to create original and novel solutions that address a problem or an opportunity

- **Discernment**: The ability to evaluate ideas and solutions using intuition, logic, and experience

- **Galvanizing**: The ability to rally others around an idea or a solution and motivate them to take action

- **Enablement**: The ability to provide the necessary resources and support to turn ideas into reality

- **Tenacity**: The ability to see things through to completion and overcome obstacles along the way

Nobody can be all of these, maybe two or three at most. You do need all of these in your organization. Lencioni's book argues that by leveraging people's affinities and skills based on these working types, you will have more productive teams, more fulfillment and joy, and improved morale across your organization. Being able to recognize and build on this knowledge will allow you to see the full potential of your team members and yourself and allow magic to happen. Never ever underestimate yourself and the people around you. All of this is rooted in the fundamental premise that nobody is perfect, and you need trust and teamwork to make the dream work.

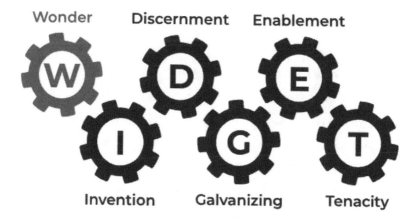

Wonder   Discernment   Enablement

Invention   Galvanizing   Tenacity

This supports the idea that you should have a team approach to your cybersecurity people strategy and program execution. You cannot expect your CISO to be a strategic thinker, high EQ leader, and have all the technical qualifications and detail-oriented rigor of a SOC analyst or system administrator. You cannot expect one person to know and do it all. In an article published by Trellix, they speak of the CISO duality where they are being pulled between two extremes: the strategic and the tactical or technical poles. CISOs should have a business acumen and understanding of your organizational business objectives and be able to communicate clearly with the leadership team in the language spoken in boardrooms, not server rooms. They need all kinds of people to execute on the cybersecurity and risk management strategy and they need the full collaboration of the leadership team and entire organization to make their cyber risk management process iterative and proactive. In short, be realistic of what you expect from any given individual, but your CISO in particular.

You may be familiar with the four DiSC profiles:

- **Dominance**: These are more strategic thinkers and results-oriented confident leaders and may be outspoken and demanding.

- **Influence**: These individuals can be enthusiastic, optimistic, open, energetic, and trusting. They place an emphasis on relationships and influencing others.

- **Steadiness**: These are the rocks in your organization; you can count on them to be dependable, cooperative, sincere, and loyal.

- **Conscientiousness**: These are the people who are detail oriented, focused on quality and accuracy, expertise, and competency.

People may lean more toward one or two shades of these profiles, and it's important to understand how to interact with them and support them in their roles. Your cybersecurity team will need all these types of complementary profiles, and together they will be successful.

When you look for a CISO, make sure there are some D, I, and S in their DiSC profile, meaning you want someone with the aptitude of a leader.

In his book *Great People Decisions: Why They Matter So Much, Why They Are So Hard, and How You Can Master Them*, Claudio Fernandez Araoz shares that people decisions are both your highest challenges and your biggest opportunity. Leaders often get people decisions wrong, in part because they delegate the decision-making to others. While others can play a role in identifying the right person for the right place, when it comes to choosing people in leadership positions, you play a very important role. Araoz also adds that most likely, the ideal candidate doesn't exist and that you have to decide which strengths are critically important versus which weaknesses are not fatal.

Lead by Example

As a leader, are you adopting and promoting the security policy that your employees have to sign and live by? Or do you get to be the exception to the rule? Do you recognize the importance of a strong security posture as it can strengthen client and partner relations and reduce the likelihood of catastrophic events? Are you learning about cybersecurity and risk management? Are you asking the CISO and your leadership team questions about risks to the business? Are you leading by example?

As business leaders, you set the tone; you embody the culture and values that represent your organization. Build a cybersecurity aware culture that people can relate to by explaining why it matters to you, the organization, and the ecosystem you operate in. If you make cybersecurity a priority, so will the rest of your organization.

As a leader, you should be aware of the burden that rests on the shoulders of your CISO. The burnout and turnover rates are extremely high in the CISO population. This is mostly due to their leadership not understanding the magnitude of the responsibilities they carry and the lack of resources they receive to manage it all. Do you care about your people and their well-being? Yes or no? It's a simple question. If you truly do, ask your CISO and their team how you can support them to build a sustainable program that won't kill them. When you invest in the well-being of your cybersecurity team, they will more likely stay when the next recruiter with a lucrative offer comes knocking on their door.

Compliance Is Not Security

Most organizations must comply with one or the other cybersecurity- and privacy-related regulation. Noncompliance can translate into

- Fines by the regulator

- Non-award of client contracts

- Loss of revenue

- In the case of the Payment Card Industry (PCI), loss of credit card transactions

- Lawsuits

These kinds of sticks make it easier to prioritize investing in compliance-based programs where holistic cybersecurity programs may seem to be more costly than what they may be worth.

However, it is absolutely critical for you to understand that every regulation is very specific to a scope and usually based on a type of data that requires the added oversight – healthcare records under HIPAA, credit card data under PCI, Controlled Unclassified Information (CUI) and Federal Contract Information (FCI) under CMMC, personal identifiable information (PII) under state privacy laws or EU's GDPR. Protecting those types of data may not necessarily prevent all breaches and a big black eye to your organization's reputation.

A few examples to make the point before weighing your investment in compliance over security:

- **Ransomware** attacks where your system's data is encrypted preventing all use of your technology have been a major source of financial losses to all types of organizations. It may just take one person clicking on a bad link or opening a file, and it's game over. Ransom payments can cost a lot, but there are no guarantees that you will get your data back nor that these malicious actors won't be coming back for more. Furthermore, usually the attackers extract data before even launching a ransomware attack, so they can get a ransom payment and sell your data on the dark web either way. According to a Varonis report, in 2024, the average cost of a ransomware attack was over $2 million.

- **Distributed Denial of Service** (DDOS) attacks are ways to overwhelm an organization's public-facing website or ecommerce site, preventing it from taking orders from clients and generating revenue. These attacks can be used as an extortion mechanism or simply to hurt someone's bottom line. With an expansive IoT infrastructure at the fingertips of malicious actors, they can now use more and more vulnerable Internet-connected devices to connect to their botnets and target whatever IP address or website the bad guys wish to target.

- Finally, the type of threat that is the most destructive and costly to recover from is **wiper malware**. NotPetya is one of those examples where it looked like ransomware, but in reality the malware which spread like wildfire across the world wiped systems down to nothing. A $10 billion hack!

Maersk, responsible for 76 ports on all sides of the earth and nearly 800 seafaring vessels, including container ships carrying tens of millions of tons of cargo, representing close to a fifth of the entire world's shipping capacity, was dead in the water when NotPetya turned everything off. If it wasn't for a random power outage in one African office sparing the last surviving domain controller, Maersk would have had to rebuild its entire global IT infrastructure, delaying the operation of this critical supply chain player even more. That was 2017.

Since then, the Russians have been targeting Ukraine with more and more variants of these destructive attacks. It is a matter of time before they expand their aperture and target more organizations and countries in their path to reaching their goals of dominance and power. If you want to learn more about the effects of cyber warfare, I recommend reading *Sandworm* by Andy Greenberg, a WIRED reporter who shares cutting-edge insights about cybercrime and warfare.

Cybercrime and its twin, cyberwar, are the number one existential threat to your business. Compliance with one or other regulation will not prevent them from ending your career.

An ounce of prevention is worth a pound of cure.

—Benjamin Franklin

Know Your Cybersecurity Risk

When you write your annual 10K report and list all the business risks, someone tells you to include a section covering cybersecurity risk and the potential exposure of a breach or operational failure caused by a cyberattack. If 10Ks are not part of your business, whether you're privately owned or a nonprofit, you do watch the news and know about cyber threats. So pleading ignorance or pretending this cyber risk is not your problem is just not an option. Our days of blissful ignorance are over.

Willful ignorance or accepting risks that could hurt your organization, partners, and clients is now a criminal act, and you will be held accountable sooner or later if you don't see cyber risk as a business risk and manage it appropriately. It will affect more people than you can imagine. If you want to learn what that could look like, see how Uber and SolarWinds had a reckoning with the SEC.

Trying to explain our current cyber risk to the board

To understand your cyber risk, the questions worth investigating are

- What are your critical business functions? What would the financial cost be if one or all of them were to go offline for a day?

- What types of data do you have and how many records of each? Fines resulting from a breach can be calculated based on the number and types of data records.

- Who are your most important vendors? Do you have a vendor risk management program in place that determines the financial risk if one of them were to be compromised?

- Who are your most valuable clients? If you were to be compromised, would this affect their loyalty and business with you? What percentage of your annual revenue does that represent?

- What is your due diligence when you hire new employees, procure from new vendors, build ventures with new partners, make new acquisitions, sell new products? Is there a risk analysis done that asks the *what if* questions?

- If someone would want to steal your intellectual property, how would they go about it? What safeguards do you have to protect your secret sauce?

None of these questions are really cybersecurity related. They are about your business and its survival or demise if you don't protect what makes it run. If someone wants to take something from you, undermine your operations, or cripple your growth, assume they will start where you can't find them.

Once you quantify the value of your critical business functions, data assets, vendors, and clients, you can understand that the investment to protect them should be appropriately allocated. Once you understand that cybersecurity is an investment where the ROI is the prevention of massive losses and protection of even greater investments, it will be a no-brainer to you and your leadership team. Cybersecurity should not be seen as a cost or overhead. It is as valuable as your most important client.

Document Your Cyber Risk Management Strategy

I highly recommend you work with your leadership team, which should include the CISO, to develop a cybersecurity risk management strategy. The NIST Risk Management Framework provides a good structure and format on how to get started with this. You and your team know what your critical business functions are and what your balance sheet and cashflow look like. You know what kind of financial losses you can tolerate and what would be a disaster.

Business disruption can be quantified in dollars and cents. Whether it's the shutdown of your ecommerce site due to a DDOS attack leading to a loss in revenue or the complete destruction of all your computers and servers due to a wiper malware like NotPetya leading to hardware replacement costs and loss in productivity – it all costs money. Cybersecurity risk is something you need to quantify in collaboration with your CISO, CFO, and business stakeholders. Your legal counsel and finance also have an idea of what your clients, partners, cyber liability insurance provider, or regulators will expect in terms of reimbursement or fines for a cybersecurity failure affecting their bottom line or the security of society and other organizations. What is your risk tolerance or appetite? Only you as a leadership team can answer that question, not the CISO.

To quantify cyber risk as FAIR prescribes it is to use a range of minimum, maximum, and most likely financial values, whether of a Single Loss Expectancy (SLE) or an Annualized Loss Expectancy (ALE) if a risk were to materialize. If you determine in advance what types of actions will be taken and how many resources will be allocated based on the potential exposure of a cyber risk, you are providing clear direction to the CISO and the business owners on how to manage risk proactively instead of reactively. Here's how this could look:

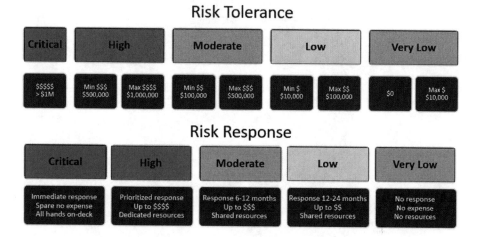

Executive Decision: Mitigate, transfer, accept or avoid risk.

The key is to maintain frequent and clear communications and use a set of metrics everyone understands and lives by. Your involvement and support in this process is absolutely critical.

Good Cybersecurity Programs Start with Good Governance

The NIST Cybersecurity Framework (CSF) is an outcomes-based framework that organizations of all sizes and in all sectors can use as a standard for their cybersecurity program. It is written in plain English and easy to understand. While the CISO in your organization is responsible for implementing many of the controls recommended by NIST, it is important to recognize that no cybersecurity program can succeed without executive buy-in and the involvement of everyone in the organization. That is why the first and overarching function of the NIST CSF is Governance.

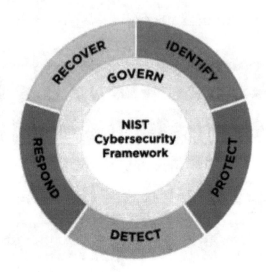

What you need to know are the main functions and what's involved with each of them in terms of the investment in people, processes, and technology. The NIST CSF functions are

- **Govern**: The organization's cybersecurity risk management strategy, expectations, and policy are established, communicated, and monitored. A cybersecurity risk management strategy is built around the organizational context, not simply your IT systems. Governance activities are critical for incorporating cybersecurity into your enterprise risk management strategy. If you and your leadership team are not involved in this process, you are setting your CISO and their program up for failure. This is why I highly recommend you and your leadership team take a NIST CSF course developed for business leaders to help you understand the roles and responsibilities you play in the development, implementation, and oversight of a successful cybersecurity risk management strategy and program.

- **Identify**: The organization's current cybersecurity risks are understood. You cannot identify risks without understanding what your assets are, their value, and the business impact if these assets were to be compromised. While most organizations have IT management systems that can identify the hardware deployed, there is a growing challenge of shadow IT sprawling in your organization that may not be on the radar. This could be Internet of Things or "smart" devices, applications not approved by acceptable use policies, or AI applications that ingest data that should not be shared with external parties. Having your business leaders involved in the identification and valuation of your business-critical functions and the assets that support the business is critical. Understanding how your partners, vendors, and customers interact with your people and systems is equally important and may require you taking a closer look at your procurement processes.

- **Protect**: Once you know what your assets are and how important they are to your organization, you can prioritize how to protect them. There are no silver bullets. Given that your most vulnerable assets are your people, you will need to implement a zero trust architecture and layer various solutions that will complement one another. These solutions include identity management, authentication, access controls, awareness and training, and data and platform security.

- **Detect**: Time is of the essence when it comes to detecting a cybersecurity attack and potential compromise or breach. There are many solutions available in this domain. Automation, machine learning, and generative AI will improve efficiencies in the detection of incidents before they become major problems.

- **Respond**: Incident response is not something you can delegate to your IT or cybersecurity people. Yes, they will be handling the technical controls to contain the effects of an incident. You actually play a critical role in the preparation and execution of a solid incident response plan. When an incident unfolds, lots of levers need to be pulled and lots of decisions need to be made with input from finance, legal, insurance, business leaders, and potentially law enforcement. Be proactive on this front and make it a priority to be as prepared as possible.

- **Recover**: Once an incident has been resolved, your organization needs to be brought back to normal operations. After everything has been said and done, the most important part is to review the incident history and identify lessons learned and areas of improvement.

Cybersecurity and risk management is an iterative process. Always ask your team: What can we do better? What are our blind spots? How can I help? You matter in this process more than you can imagine. Own it.

How You Respond to Adversity Matters

Shit will hit the fan. There is no doubt about it: you will get hacked. Actually, the C-suite is a prime social engineering target! How the CEO handles an incident or a breach and treats their team during these stressful times can determine whether or not your organization survives the event or the next. Here's why good leadership matters in the face of cyber threats and business disruption:

- Your team will need your direction during the incident response planning stages and the actual incident response.

- If you have gone through incident response tabletop exercises, you know that you are responsible for declaring an incident. You are responsible for activating the resources needed to respond to and recover from an incident.

- Your participation is mandatory. You have to be present and not delay your participation in the preparation or response to an incident.

- You are the face of the company, and how you represent yourself and update your organization's stakeholders, internal or external, will be scrutinized very carefully.

- Learn from the lessons an incident taught you. Do you need more resources, is there a gap in your process, do you and your people need more specialized training, do you need to strengthen some security controls, technical, administrative, or others? Lots of questions should be asked during this process, and decisions need to be made on how to adjust your cybersecurity posture and address newly identified risks.

- If during the aftermath you have to explain who or what was responsible, don't throw your CISO and their team under the bus. Own up to your ultimate responsibility to protect the best interests of your organization and its stakeholders. The buck stops with you.

- Don't forget to thank your team and reward them for their investment of time and energy when you needed them the most. When times get tough and budgets need to be cut, avoid cutting your cybersecurity team's budget. You cannot afford to lose them.

Taking on a challenge is a lot like riding a horse. If you're comfortable while doing it, you're probably doing it wrong.

—Ted Lasso

Who has the time amidst all this chaos?

Most Importantly, Build Trust

All of the above matters. But it won't matter at all if people don't trust you. To be a successful leader, you must build a culture where everyone has a voice and where mistakes can be made and learned from. It begins and ends with you. If you cannot admit to your team that you are not perfect and that you are not better or smarter than them, you are destined to fail. Your mindset will determine how far you can take your organization.

In Patrick Lencioni's book, *The Five Dysfunctions of a Team*, trust is the foundation of everything. Without trust, there is no winning; there is no us. The five dysfunctions or five symptoms of a dysfunctional team Lencioni speaks of are

- Absence of trust

- Fear of conflict

- Lack of commitment

- Avoidance of accountability

- Poor results

A high-performing team on the other hand demonstrates

- Trust and the ability to be vulnerable and ask for help

- Healthy debates and collaboration

- Engaged and committed team members

- Ownership and accountability from the top down and within a team

- Focus on team results and a motivation to succeed

You need to build a culture where people can bring their best to work and where they are appreciated and recognized for their contributions and unique qualities. Keep a people-first mentality where every problem has a solution, and together you can come up with creative ways to solve them. Believe that your people can overcome any challenge, and they will believe you.

If you treat your employees like they make a difference, they will.

—Jim Goodnight, CEO & Co-Founder of SAS Institute

CHAPTER 11

Let's Wrap It Up

You Matter

Every single human is equally vulnerable to cybercrime, yet they also are equally powerful in keeping themselves and each other safe. You matter in the equation of us versus them.

There aren't enough cybersecurity experts to keep us all safe from cybercrime. There is a talent gap that we seem to inflict on ourselves for some reason or another. You can't delegate the safety of your family to the few. You and everyone around you have to play a part in the solution that keeps us all safe. The more we all are aware of the threats, whether they're lurking from the dark web or just your social media feed, the better we can avoid the risk of harm, physical, financial, or emotional.

Most importantly, cybersecurity is not just about keeping your personal data, identity, and finances safe. It is about you maintaining your freedom and free will. How you think, feel, or act should be driven by your personal values, goals, and beliefs. The question we need to ask ourselves: Is that currently the case or is someone else steering the ship?

© Cathy Olieslaeger 2025
C. Olieslaeger, *Cybersecurity for Everyone*, Apress Pocket Guides,
https://doi.org/10.1007/979-8-8688-1408-2_11

Zero Trust

In a technology-driven society where we are digital personas with a digital footprint, you must adopt a zero-trust approach to protect yourself, your family, and community.

- Do not trust the technology you own to protect you, your kids, and parents. Assume that the technology providers want to maximize their profits. Your safety and well-being do not support their financial goals.

- Do not trust free applications that do not explain what problems they solve. The application is not their product, you are, every bit and byte, every one and zero.

- Do not trust the content that you see to be true, whether you searched for it or it was served to you during your scroll of doom.

- Do not trust the representatives in government to represent your best interests as long as their campaigns and retirement savings are funded by the companies who profit off of your existence and adoption of their technology.

In a capitalistic economy where greedy billionaires have a say on how a country is governed, your best interests, privacy, and safety are not as important as their financial gains. You and your well-being aren't important at all.

That said, you can control what you share with the world, which technology you use, which apps you download, and where you find information. These actions should be driven by your awareness of the macro dynamics and online threats as well as by fact-based information you gain from a variety of sources, preferably not just local or regional. You may learn a thing or two from listening to international news sources.

Control Your Reality

You control how you protect yourself and those you care about. These are a few simple tricks that don't have to cost much money or time. Here's a recap:

- First, freeze your credit.

- Use a password manager that has a strong reputation and a two-step authentication (2FA) process.

- Use two-factor authentication (2FA) on all apps and websites you use, including social media, ecommerce sites like your grocer or Amazon, banking and investment apps, healthcare provider portals, email, drives or cloud backups of your mobile device, etc.

- Create a passcode or question/answer that you and your family share to authenticate each other in case someone uses your voice to coerce your family to pay money to bail you out of jail or some other weird emergency.

- Update the operating system, software, and applications on all your devices on a regular basis. That should include all the smart devices hanging around your house.

- Use encryption if available.

- Deny all cookies and tracking by websites or mobile apps.

- Minimize the applications on your devices to those you absolutely must use.

- Avoid social media.

- Avoid scrolls of videos that you did not subscribe to.

- Get your news from a variety of sources from a variety of places.

- Report any scams you are the victim of.

- Share lessons learned with your friends, family, and colleagues.

Join the Cyber Hero Squad

I painted a pretty stark picture of the crazy world we live in. Consider joining the Cyber Hero Squad and making it your purpose to protect the greater good. Whether you wish to have your hands on a keyboard, your eyes on glass, or be the leader supporting an organization in managing their cybersecurity risk strategy. There are a million and one opportunities to leverage your strengths, insights, and experiences no matter what your background is. You can make a real difference.

Breaking into cybersecurity may have its challenges. Here are a few hacks to overcome these brick walls:

- Find your tribe. Join a local association and attend networking events and competitions.

- Embrace mentorship. Find a mentor or two and be a mentor as soon as you've been around the block.

- Be resourceful. There are lots of free educational content available in books, blogs, vlogs, podcasts, courses, etc.

- Discover the various paths available to you during internships. Experience matters.

- Participate in Capture the Flag or other competitions to get a feel for the technical aspects of cybersecurity.

- If you're not really a techno geek but geeky enough to like cybersecurity, consider specializing in Governance, Risk, and Compliance. Why not be a CISO or a business leader who considers cybersecurity a business enabler?

- Share your lessons learned.

- Leverage your durable skills. Grow your emotional intelligence.

- Recognize that there is bias in the system and find ways to avoid or address it. But don't let it stop you!

- Pay it forward. Help the next kid in line. Be a mentor, a role model, a public speaker...

- Inspire others to join us and beat the bad guys.

We are all one. Only egos, beliefs, and fears separate us.

—Nikola Tesla

Resources

Throughout this book, I shared many resources that I hope you consult on your journey into cybersecurity. Whether you are a student, professional, teacher, or parent, there are many sources you can leverage to complement this "pocket guide."

I hope this helps you be smarter, stronger, and more resilient in the face of all this technological innovation and the dangers lurking around its corners.

I strongly believe that together we can rewrite the people story in cybersecurity. It starts and ends with you and me. Let's do it. We got this!

Start with Why

- TED, How Great Leaders Inspire Action, Simon Sinek

    - https://www.ted.com/talks/simon_sinek_how_
      great_leaders_inspire_action?subtitle=en

- Book: Start with Why, Simon Sinek

    - https://www.goodreads.com/book/show/7108725-
      start-with-why

- Video: Think Different, Steve Jobs

    - https://youtu.be/GEPhLqwKo6g?si=Uh_
      7ZiI4mCtSix27

- North Dakota Computer Science and Cybersecurity
  Standard

    - https://www.nd.gov/dpi/sites/www/files/
      documents/Academic%20Support/CSCS2019.pdf

- HB 1398 becomes law in North Dakota in 2023

    - https://www.k12dive.com/news/north-dakota-
      first-cybersecurity-education/646340/

- Video/Podcast: Diary of a CEO, Simon Sinek,
  episode 230

    - https://youtu.be/D46zvJI-njU?si=tlKqKo
      NkTSkJa_No

Journey into Cybersecurity

- The Triangle Net LLC

    - `https://www.TheTriangleNet.com`

- Podcast, Journey into Cybersecurity

    - `https://www.buzzsprout.com/1750617/follow`

Common Misconceptions

- The Global Risks Report 2024, World Economic Forum

    - `https://www3.weforum.org/docs/WEF_The_`
      `Global_Risks_Report_2024.pdf`

We're Losing

- FBI Internet Crime Report: IC3 Annual Report

    - `https://www.ic3.gov/`

- Crowdstrike Global Threat Report

    - `https://www.crowdstrike.com/adversaries/`

- Google: Mandiant's M-Trends Report

    - `https://cloud.google.com/security/`
      `resources/m-trends`

- The Verizon Data Breach Investigations Report (DBIR)

    - `https://www.verizon.com/business/resources/`
      `reports/dbir/`

- Palo Alto Unit 42 Incident Response Report

  - https://unit42.paloaltonetworks.com/

- IBM Cost of a Data Breach Report

  - https://www.ibm.com/reports/data-breach

- Book: The Sisterhood: The Secret History of Women at the CIA, Liza Mundy

  - https://www.goodreads.com/book/show/81360005-the-sisterhood

  - https://www.goodreads.com/book/show/46015931-women-know-cyber

- Video: Women Know Cyber

  - https://youtu.be/Kpc31WJ6l2M?si=vMfD5YRrFufCZxpT

- Book: Women Know Cyber: 100 Fascinating Females Fighting Cybercrime, Steve Morgan and Di Freeze

  - https://cybersecurityventures.com/women-know-cyber-100-fascinating-females-fighting-cybercrime/

  - https://www.goodreads.com/book/show/46015931-women-know-cyber

- Video: TED Talk, Why are women still taken less seriously than men? Mary Ann Sieghart

  - https://www.ted.com/talks/mary_ann_sieghart_why_are_women_still_taken_less_seriously_than_men

- MGM Casino hack

    - `https://www.youtube.com/watch?v=ZVCvqp4Rz0Q`

- HBR, Why Women Don't Apply for Jobs Unless They're 100% Qualified

    - `https://hbr.org/2014/08/why-women-dont-apply-for-jobs-unless-theyre-100-qualified`

- Video: TED Talk, I am a Fraud; I think you're a fraud, too, Melissa Hughes

    - `https://www.ted.com/talks/melissa_hughes_i_am_a_fraud_i_think_you_re_a_fraud_too`

- The Circuit: The dark side of AI is already here. S1 E7, Emily Chang, Bloomberg, July 28, 2023

    - `https://www.bloomberg.com/news/audio/2023-07-28/whistleblowers-warn-about-the-dark-side-of-ai-podcast`

    - `https://youtu.be/QHlacIwhZVo?si=nCoqKN24Y8zsHZe8`

- Types of bias, Wikipedia

    - `https://en.wikipedia.org/wiki/Bias`

- Google, Microsoft, and Perplexity Are Promoting Scientific Racism in Search Results, WIRED

    - `https://www.wired.com/story/google-microsoft-perplexity-scientific-racism-search-results-ai/`

- The Matrix scene with the red and blue pill

    - `https://youtu.be/zE7PKRjrid4?si=eNPpYKaoEQqlx9jp`

How Does Cybercrime Affect You and Your Family?

- Internet Crime Complaint Center, IC3

    - https://www.ic3.gov/

- FBI Public Service Announcement issued on July 18, 2023: Increase in Tech Support Scams Targeting Older Adults and Directing Victims to Send Cash through Shipping Companies

    - https://www.ic3.gov/PSA/2023/PSA230718

- FBI Public Service Announcement issued on November 17, 2023: FBI Warns of Scammers Targeting Senior Citizens in Grandparent Scams and Demanding Funds by Wire, Mail, or Couriers

    - https://www.ic3.gov/PSA/2023/PSA231117

- FBI Public Service Announcement issued on March 14, 2023: The FBI Warns of a Spike in Cryptocurrency Investment Schemes

    - https://www.ic3.gov/PSA/2023/PSA230314

- FBI Public Service Announcement issued on June 5, 2023: Malicious Actors Manipulating Photos and Videos to Create Explicit Content and Sextortion Schemes

    - https://www.ic3.gov/PSA/2023/PSA230605

- FBI Public Service Announcement issued on October 24, 2023: Scammers Solicit Fake Humanitarian Donations

    - https://www.ic3.gov/PSA/2023/PSA231024

- FBI Public Service Announcement issued on October 18, 2024: Just So You Know: Foreign Threat Actors Likely to Use a Variety of Tactics to Develop and Spread Disinformation During 2024 U.S. General Election Cycle

    - https://www.ic3.gov/PSA/2024/PSA241018

- FBI Public Service Announcement issued on June 24, 2024: Fictitious Law Firms Targeting Cryptocurrency Scam Victims Offering to Recover Funds

    - https://www.ic3.gov/PSA/2024/PSA240624

- Guide on 5 Common LinkedIn Scams, Tripwire

    - https://www.tripwire.com/state-of-security/a-guide-on-5-common-linkedin-scams

- Podcast: Darknet Diaries, Episode 142, Axact (Degree fraud)

    - https://darknetdiaries.com/transcript/142/

- FTC Consumer Advice, College Degree Scams

    - https://consumer.ftc.gov/articles/college-degree-scams

- FTC Consumer Advice, Student Loan and Education Scams

    - https://consumer.ftc.gov/all-scams/student-loan-education-scams

- Office for Civil Rights, Breaches of unsecured protected health information affecting 500 or more individuals

  - https://ocrportal.hhs.gov/ocr/breach/breach_report.jsf

- What Is a Data Broker, McAfee

  - https://www.mcafee.com/blogs/tips-tricks/what-is-a-data-broker/

- What Are Data Brokers, Discover

  - https://www.discover.com/credit-cards/card-smarts/what-are-data-brokers/

- National Public Data, the hacked data broker that lost millions of Social Security numbers and more, files for bankruptcy, TechCrunch, October 14, 2024

  - https://techcrunch.com/2024/10/14/national-public-data-the-hacked-data-broker-that-lost-millions-of-social-security-numbers-and-more-files-for-bankruptcy/

- The Global Surveillance Free-for-All in Mobile Ad Data, Krebs on Security, October 2024

  - https://krebsonsecurity.com/2024/10/the-global-surveillance-free-for-all-in-mobile-ad-data/

- OCR Wall of Shame

  - https://ocrportal.hhs.gov/ocr/breach/breach_report.jsf

- US DHHS: FAQ Change Healthcare Cybersecurity Incident

  - `https://www.hhs.gov/hipaa/for-professionals/special-topics/change-healthcare-cybersecurity-incident-frequently-asked-questions/index.html`

- 23andMe pledges $30 million to the 6.4 million people affected by data breach, The Record, September 13, 2024

  - `https://therecord.media/dna-pledges-millions-to-data-breach`

- UK National Health System (NHS) Attacks

  - `https://www.databreachtoday.co.uk/uk-health-records-breached-18-million-a-5261`

  - `https://www.bbc.com/news/articles/c9ww90j9dj8o`

- HC3 releases threat profile on Qilin ransomware targeting global healthcare, other critical sectors, June 2024

  - `https://industrialcyber.co/medical/hc3-releases-threat-profile-on-qilin-ransomware-targeting-global-healthcare-other-critical-sectors/`

- PCI Data Security Standard

  - `https://www.pcisecuritystandards.org/standards/`

- Verizon Annual Payment Security Report

  - `https://www.verizon.com/business/reports/payment-security-report/`

- Five Biggest PCI Breaches

  - `https://www.goanywhere.com/blog/the-5-biggest-pci-compliance-breaches`

- ProofPoint: Lessons Learned from Heartland Breach

  - `https://www.proofpoint.com/us/blog/insider-threat-management/throwback-thursday-lessons-learned-2008-heartland-breach`

- An Interview With the Target & Home Depot Hacker, Krebs on Security, November 2024

  - `https://krebsonsecurity.com/2024/11/an-interview-with-the-target-home-depot-hacker/`

- Robert Cialdini's Six Principles of Persuasion

  - `https://youtu.be/cFdCzN7RYbw`

  - `https://www.netreputation.com/cialdinis-6-principles-of-persuasion/`

- Groupthink

  - `https://corporatefinanceinstitute.com/resources/management/groupthink-decisions/`

- Dotcom Bubble

  - `https://www.investopedia.com/terms/d/dotcom-bubble.asp`

- Real Estate Bubble
  - `https://www.investopedia.com/ask/answers/100314/when-did-real-estate-bubble-burst.asp`
- Crypto Currency Bubble
  - `https://www.investopedia.com/news/cryptocurrency-bubble-more-housing-or-dotcom/`
- Nazi Propaganda
  - `https://encyclopedia.ushmm.org/content/en/article/nazi-propaganda`
- Newly Published Cambridge Analytica Documents Show Unlawful Support for Trump in 2016, October 16, 2020
  - `https://campaignlegal.org/update/newly-published-cambridge-analytica-documents-show-unlawful-support-trump-2016`
- 'The Great Hack': Cambridge Analytica is just the tip of the iceberg, July 24, 2019
  - `https://www.amnesty.org/en/latest/news/2019/07/the-great-hack-facebook-cambridge-analytica/`
- Global Conflict Tracker
  - `https://www.cfr.org/global-conflict-tracker/conflict/conflict-ukraine`
- Video: Hearing, The threat of China to America's Critical Infrastructure, January 31, 2024
  - `https://selectcommitteeontheccp.house.gov/about/events/hearing-ccp-cyber-threat-american-homeland-and-national-security`

- CISA: People's Republic of China Cyber Threat

  - https://www.cisa.gov/topics/cyber-threats-
    and-advisories/nation-state-cyber-actors/
    china

- CISA: Nation-State Cyber Actors

  - https://www.cisa.gov/topics/cyber-threats-
    and-advisories/nation-state-cyber-actors

- Joint Statement from FBI and CISA on the People's
  Republic of China (PRC) Targeting of Commercial
  Telecommunications Infrastructure, November 13, 2024

  - https://www.cisa.gov/news-events/news/
    joint-statement-fbi-and-cisa-peoples-
    republic-china-prc-targeting-commercial-
    telecommunications

- United Nations Office of Drugs and Crime, Handbook
  on Children Recruited and Exploited by Terrorist and
  Violent Extremist Groups, 2017

  - https://www.unodc.org/documents/justice-
    and-prison-reform/Child-Victims/Handbook_
    on_Children_Recruited_and_Exploited_
    by_Terrorist_and_Violent_Extremist_Groups_
    the_Role_of_the_Justice_System.E.pdf

- Video: Documenting Hate: New American Nazis, PBS
  Frontline, 2018

  - https://youtu.be/-XFBVAAzXjc?si=tGtCKeUaLu
    Uwzyn4

- Video: American Terror: The Military's Problem With
  Extremism in the Ranks, VICE News, 2022

- `https://youtu.be/lVkBVExuXSQ?si=57IWD 1a7gAfDqN9C`

- Meta drops fact checkers in US, what does this mean for the world?, Context, Thomson Reuters Foundation, January 16, 2025

  - `https://www.context.news/big-tech/meta-drops-fact-checkers-in-us-what-does-this-mean-for-the-world`

- Meta eliminates fact-checking in latest bow to Trump, AP, January 2025

  - `https://apnews.com/article/meta-facts-trump-musk-community-notes-413b8495939a058f f2d25fd23f2e0f43`

- Inside Facebook, Jan. 6 violence fueled anger, regret over missed warning signs, Washington Post, October 22, 2021

  - `https://www.washingtonpost.com/technology/ 2021/10/22/jan-6-capitol-riot-facebook/`

- What the Jan. 6 probe found out about social media, but didn't report, Washington Post, January 17, 2023

  - `https://www.washingtonpost.com/technology/ 2023/01/17/jan6-committee-report-social-media/`

- Select January 6th Committee Final Report and Supporting Materials Collection

  - `https://www.govinfo.gov/collection/ january-6th-committee-final-report?path=/GPO/ January%206th%20Committee%20Final%20Report%20 and%20Supporting%20Materials%20Collection`

- Trump- and Musk-fueled falsehoods and threats backdrop US election, The Guardian, November 5, 2024

    - https://www.theguardian.com/us-news/2024/nov/05/election-trump-musk-misinformation-false-claims

- Disinformation from adversaries and Americans swamped 2024 election, The Hill, November 8, 2024

    - https://thehill.com/national-security/4979502-2024-election-disinformation-impact/

- DHS: National Terrorism Advisory, May 24, 2023

    - https://www.dhs.gov/ntas/advisory/national-terrorism-advisory-system-bulletin-may-24-2023

- GAO: The Rising Threat of Domestic Terrorism in the U.S. and Federal Efforts to Combat It

    - https://www.gao.gov/blog/rising-threat-domestic-terrorism-u.s.-and-federal-efforts-combat-it

How to Keep You and Your Family Safe

- WIRED: 9 Best Password Managers

    - https://www.wired.com/story/best-password-managers/

- Secure our World, How to Keep your Family Safe, CISA

    - https://www.cisa.gov/secure-our-world

- How to help families keep children safe online, eSafety, Australia's independent regulator for online safety

    - `https://www.esafety.gov.au/communities/`
      `child-safe-communities/families`

- Forbes, Microsoft Confirms Password Deletion For 1 Billion Users—Attacks Up 200%, December 13, 2024

    - `https://www.forbes.com/sites/`
      `zakdoffman/2024/12/13/microsoft-confirms-`
      `password-deletion-for-1-billion-users-`
      `attacks-up-200/`

- Microsoft blog: Convincing a billion users to love passkeys: UX design insights from Microsoft to boost adoption and security (Identity and Access Management Best Practices)

    - `https://www.microsoft.com/en-us/security/`
      `blog/2024/12/12/convincing-a-billion-users-`
      `to-love-passkeys-ux-design-insights-from-`
      `microsoft-to-boost-adoption-and-security/`

- Yubico, How the YubiKey Works

    - `https://www.yubico.com/products/how-the-`
      `yubikey-works/`

- Resources on how to manage sextortion

    - `https://www.missingkids.org/theissues/`
      `sextortion#resources`

- Podcast: Darknet Diaries, "The Pig Butcher"

    - `https://darknetdiaries.com/episode/141/`

- Video: Last Week Tonight with John Oliver, Pig Butchering Scams

  - `https://youtu.be/pLPpl2ISKTg?si=pDfxV3QwGJkKzFgo`

- Video: Bloomberg Investigates, How YouTube Scambaiters Turn the Tables on Internet Fraud

  - `https://youtu.be/Cj_9Ix_6pK8?si=zdprBK21RCiQg61M`

- MissingKids.org, Sextortion

  - `https://www.missingkids.org/theissues/sextortion`

- These Apps Collect the Most Personal Data

  - `https://www.pcmag.com/news/sick-of-data-collection-try-these-apps-instead`

- Blue Campaign, Human Trafficking Awareness Campaign by the DHS

  - `https://www.dhs.gov/blue-campaign`

- Human Trafficking Data Collection Activities, 2023

  - `https://bjs.ojp.gov/library/publications/human-trafficking-data-collection-activities-2023`

- Freeze your Credit

  - Equifax

    - `https://www.equifax.com/personal/credit-report-services/credit-freeze/`

- Experian

  - https://www.experian.com/freeze/center.html

- TransUnion

  - https://www.transunion.com/credit-freeze

- DeleteMe

  - https://www.deleteme.com/

- Atlas Data Privacy

  - https://www.atlas.net/

- Recorded Future blog, DNS Servers

  - https://www.recordedfuture.com/threat-intelligence-101/cyber-threat-landscape/dns-servers

- CleanBrowsing, DNS-based content filtering

  - https://cleanbrowsing.org/filters/

- The Global Surveillance Free-for-All in Mobile Ad Data, Krebs on Security, October 2024

  - https://krebsonsecurity.com/2024/10/the-global-surveillance-free-for-all-in-mobile-ad-data/

- What you really sign up for when you use social media, CNBC, May 2015

  - https://www.cnbc.com/2015/05/20/what-you-really-sign-up-for-when-you-use-social-media.html

Plan of Action for Educators

- Minimize exposure to cyberattacks and build secure and resilient K-12 cyber systems

    - https://www.schoolsafety.gov/cybersecurity

- A Glossary of Common Cybersecurity Words and Phrases, NICCS

    - https://niccs.cisa.gov/cybersecurity-career-resources/vocabulary

- Podcast: Journey into Cybersecurity

    - Video: Start with why: https://youtu.be/_pZzMiXO5yQ

    - Video: Words of Wisdom: https://youtu.be/GOZJTsajeKk

- Cybersecurity card games created by CIAS UTSA

    - https://www.youtube.com/@ciasutsa587

    - First game, How to Play Cyber Threat Guardian: https://www.youtube.com/watch?v=KiuhZfVvuko

    - Second game, How to Play Cyber Threat Protector: https://www.youtube.com/watch?v=CkD--gdkYgo

    - Third game to play at home, How to Play Cyber Threat Defender: https://www.youtube.com/watch?v=WJ76DydwejI

- Videos for kids: "We can secure our world!"

    - How to make strong passwords

        https://youtu.be/XXrbut5xRbE?si=udPlbFYTfvUE4S4V

- How to turn on MFA

  https://youtu.be/QWwaidg3AtY?si=MDdKoT-
  7X8Oblzro

- How to avoid phishing

  https://youtu.be/sgOkQYvTlnc?si=rYOQnc
  lLzl8SJbGl

- How to update software

  https://youtu.be/zCcX6aSXcLI?si=gQd9
  dL71hEJdDnfE

- Video on online privacy for kids

  - https://youtu.be/yiKeLOKc1tw?si=FGojOI
    qWiyn9wiVV

- Video for teens on healthy relationships

  - https://youtu.be/ldjZCvqhNWw

- Videos and quizzes on Khan Academy on cybersecurity

  - https://www.khanacademy.org/partner-
    content/nova/nova-labs-topic/cyber/v/
    cybersecurity-101

- Book: Cybersecurity for Teens, an Activity Book,
  Dfour Press

- Book: Cybersecurity for Teens: Learn the Terms,
  Daniel Amadi

- Book: See Yourself in Cybersecurity, Zinet Kemal

- CTF: https://hackchallengesforkids.com/

- TryHackMe CTF: https://tryhackme.com/

- Phishing Quiz: `https://www.sonicwall.com/phishing-iq-test/`

- The Triangle Net: K-12 Teacher resources

  - `https://www.thetrianglenet.com/high-school-cyber-program/`

- CyberStart America

  - `https://www.nationalcyberscholarship.org/programs/cyberstartamerica`

  - `https://www.nationalcyberscholarship.org/`

- K12 Resources for Cybersecurity Education at Home, NICE

  - `https://nicek12athome.weebly.com/`

- K12 Cybersecurity Education Community of Interest, NICE

  - `https://www.nist.gov/itl/applied-cybersecurity/nice/community/community-coordinating-council/k12-cybersecurity-education`

- NICE Cybersecurity Career Awareness Week in October

  - `https://www.nist.gov/itl/applied-cybersecurity/nice/events/cybersecurity-career-week`

- Free CIAS Card Games

  - `https://cias.utsa.edu/k-12/`

- The Last Mile Education Fund

  - `https://www.lastmile-ed.org/`

- NCWIT Resources for Educators

  - `https://ncwit.org/k-12/`

- CYBER.ORG Cyber Safety Videos

  - `https://cyber.org/cybersafety`

- NCyTE Center Cybersecurity Curriculum

  - `https://www.ncyte.net/faculty/cybersecurity-curriculum`

- NICCS Education and Training Catalog

  - `https://niccs.cisa.gov/education-training/catalog`

- GenCyber

  - `https://public.cyber.mil/gencyber/`

- High School Cybersecurity Workshop

  - `https://www.hscybersecurity.org/teachers`

- CyberPatriot

  - `https://www.uscyberpatriot.org/`

  - `https://www.youtube.com/user/CyberPatriotAFA/videos`

- Microsoft High School Program

  - `https://careers.microsoft.com/v2/global/en/discoveryprogram`

- Microsoft for Educators

  - `https://learn.microsoft.com/en-us/training/educator-center/`

- Annual IBM Report: Cost of a Breach
    - `https://www.ibm.com/reports/data-breach`
- Annual Verizon Data Breach Investigations Report
    - `https://www.verizon.com/business/resources/reports/dbir/`
- Durable Skills website
    - `https://durableskills.org/`
- Podcast: Journey into Cybersecurity, Adrianne George
    - `https://www.youtube.com/watch?v=AuNHenu3CQ8`
- Podcast/Short: Journey into Cybersecurity, Antonio Chousa answers the question what schools should offer
    - `https://youtube.com/shorts/A9QPrEHzUJg?si=w1ELtGjL5zcIw_S-`

Plan of Action for Students

- CyberSeek Interactive Map
    - `https://www.cyberseek.org/heatmap.html`
- CyberSeek Career Pathway
    - `https://www.cyberseek.org/pathway.html`
- Associations: Find your tribe
    - ISSA
        - `https://www.issa.org/`
    - ISACA
        - `https://www.isaca.org/`

- (ISC)2

  - https://www.isc2.org/

- OWASP

  - https://owasp.org/

- WiCyS

  - https://www.wicys.org/

- CSA

  - https://cloudsecurityalliance.org/

- Find your Tribe, The Triangle Net website

  - https://www.thetrianglenet.com/join-us/

- The Triangle Net, Mentorships

  - https://www.thetrianglenet.com/mentorships-internships-jobs/

- ISSA AIM (Apprenticeships, Internships, and Mentorships)

  - https://www.issa.org/what-is-aim-program/

- Book: Pathfinders, Navigating Your Career Map with a Personal Board of Advisors, Pete Schramm

  - https://golattitude.com/pathfinders-book/

- Podcasts

  - Darknet Diaries

    - https://darknetdiaries.com/

  - The CyberWire

    - https://thecyberwire.com/

- Journey into Cybersecurity
  - `https://www.thetrianglenet.com/journey-into-cybersecurity/`
- The Triangle Net resources
  - `https://www.thetrianglenet.com/resources/`
- Raleigh InfoSeCon Recordings of Presentations
  - `https://www.triangleinfosecon.com/`
  - `https://www.youtube.com/@RaleighISSA`
- The Triangle Net Educational Resources
  - `https://www.thetrianglenet.com/learning/`
- CompTIA Security+
  - `https://www.comptia.org/certifications/security`
- (ISC)2 Certified in Cybersecurity
  - `https://www.isc2.org/certifications/cc`
- Google Cybersecurity Certificate
  - `https://grow.google/certificates/cybersecurity/`
- Professor Messer YouTube
  - `https://www.youtube.com/professormesser`
- Microsoft security training
  - `https://learn.microsoft.com/en-us/training/`
- Microsoft Zero Trust description
  - `https://www.microsoft.com/en-us/videoplayer/embed/RE4J3ms?postJsllMsg=true`

- Cyber degrees

  - `https://www.cyberdegrees.org/`

- NIST CSF

  - `https://nvlpubs.nist.gov/nistpubs/CSWP/NIST.CSWP.29.pdf`

- CIS Top 18

  - `https://www.cisecurity.org/controls/cis-controls-list`

- HIPAA regulations

  - `https://www.hhs.gov/hipaa/for-professionals/index.html`

- PCI DSS

  - `https://www.pcisecuritystandards.org/`

- EU GDPR

  - `https://gdpr.eu/what-is-gdpr/`

- California's Consumer Privacy Act (CCPA)

  - `https://oag.ca.gov/privacy/ccpa`

- ISACA CISM

  - `https://www.isaca.org/credentialing/cism`

- (ISC)2 certifications incl. CISSP

  - `https://www.isc2.org/Certifications`

- GRC Learning Resources

  - `https://www.thetrianglenet.com/grc/`

- Simply Cyber, The Definitive GRC Analyst Program

  - `https://academy.simplycyber.io/p/the-definitive-grc-analyst-program`

- NICCS Cyber Career Pathways Tool

  - `https://niccs.cisa.gov/workforce-development/cyber-career-pathways-tool?selected-role=OG-WRL-009`

- SANS 20 Coolest Careers in Cyber

  - `https://www.sans.org/cybersecurity-careers/20-coolest-cyber-security-careers/`

- Pathways, cyber enabling jobs

  - `https://public.cyber.mil/wid/pathways/`

- How to Be an Ethical Hacker in 2025, TCM Security

  - `https://tcm-sec.com/how-to-be-an-ethical-hacker-in-2025/`

- Durable Skills

  - `https://durableskills.org/`

- Video: The 4 domains of emotional intelligence, Daniel Goleman

  - `https://youtu.be/erfgEHHfFkU?si=MYt5Yr rqIlZBb2Ul`

- Book: Emotional Intelligence: Why It Can Matter More than IQ, Daniel Goleman

  - `https://www.goodreads.com/book/show/26329. Emotional_Intelligence?ref=nav_sb_ss_1_54`

- Book: Focus: The Hidden Driver of Excellence,
  Daniel Goleman

  - `https://www.goodreads.com/book/show/`
    `17349126-focus?ref=nav_sb_ss_2_20`

- Book: Emotional Intelligence 2.0, Travis Bradberry and
  Jean Graves

  - `https://www.goodreads.com/book/show/6486483-`
    `emotional-intelligence-2-0?ref=nav_`
    `sb_ss_1_26`

- Book: The Five Dysfunctions of a Team, Patrick
  Lencioni

  - `https://www.goodreads.com/book/show/21343.`
    `The_Five_Dysfunctions_of_a_Team?ref=nav_`
    `sb_ss_1_31`

- Video: What Is Trust Actually?, Simon Sinek

  - `https://youtu.be/wz1vmOjae2O?si=eYlbO`
    `VS3sH6ipDm6`

- GenCyber Camps for Students

  - `https://public.cyber.mil/gencyber/`
    `camp-catalog/`

- Capture the Flag

  - TryHackMe: `https://tryhackme.com/`

  - HackTheBox: `https://www.hackthebox.com/`
    `hacker/ctf`

  - Pico CTF: `https://picoctf.org/`

- Internships
  - The Triangle Net Internships
    - `https://www.thetrianglenet.com/mentorships-internships-jobs/`
  - Indeed Internships
    - `https://www.indeed.com/jobs?q=cyber+security+internship&l=United+States&vjk=d01743f2aec49887`
  - LinkedIn Internships
    - `https://www.internships.com`
  - Apprenticeships
    - `https://www.apprenticeship.gov/`
  - ISSA AIM (Apprenticeships, Internships, and Mentorships)
    - `https://www.issa.org/what-is-aim-program/`
  - CompTIA Apprenticeships
    - `https://www.comptia.org/content/lp/apprenticeships-for-tech`
  - Microsoft Student Programs
    - `https://careers.microsoft.com/v2/global/en/programs/students.html`
  - Handshake for Students
    - `https://joinhandshake.com/students/`

- Scholarships

  - The Triangle Net Scholarship Listing

    - `https://www.thetrianglenet.com/scholarships/`

  - WiCyS scholarships for girls and women

    - `https://www.wicys.org/initiatives/programs/`

  - (ISC)2 and Center for Cyber Safety and Education

    - `https://www.iamcybersafe.org/s/scholarships`

  - ISSA

    - `https://issaef.org/scholarships/apply/`

- CSO, Women in Cyber Day finds those it celebrates 'leaving in droves'

  - `https://www.csoonline.com/article/3499360/women-in-cyber-day-finds-those-it-celebrates-leaving-in-droves.html/amp/`

- Video: Women Know Cyber

  - `https://youtu.be/Kpc31WJ6l2M?si=vMfD5YRrFufCZxpT`

- Book: Women Know Cyber: 100 Fascinating Females Fighting Cybercrime, Steve Morgan and Di Freeze

  - `https://cybersecurityventures.com/women-know-cyber-100-fascinating-females-fighting-cybercrime/`

  - `https://www.goodreads.com/book/show/46015931-women-know-cyber`

- Women in CyberSecurity (WiCyS)

    - `https://www.wicys.org/`

- "The Last Lecture" by Randy Pausch

    - Book: `https://www.goodreads.com/book/show/40611510-the-last-lecture`

    - Video: `https://youtu.be/ji5_MqicxSo?si=8T59Jrnn-JlKL7ud`

- Women in Cybersecurity Associations

    - `https://www.thetrianglenet.com/women-in-cybersecurity/`

- Ted Lasso, Believe!

    - `https://youtu.be/olPLvuvMcSE?si=WoI6eRCmPAOHD-QJ`

- Book: Cybersecurity Career Master Plan: Proven Techniques and Effective Tips to Help You Advance in Your Cybersecurity Career, Dr. Gerald Auger, Jaclyn "Jax" Scott, Jonathan Helmus, Kim Nguyen

    - `https://www.goodreads.com/book/show/58961354-cybersecurity-career-master-plan`

- Book: Navigating the Cybersecurity Career Path, Helen E. Patton

    - `https://www.wiley.com/en-us/Navigating+the+Cybersecurity+Career+Path-p-9781119833437`

- Book: The Struggle Is Real: A Blueprint to Excelling Into The Cybersecurity Discipline, Katia Dean

    - `https://katiascylife.tech/book/`

Plan of Action for Hiring Managers and HR Leaders

- 8 Tips for Hiring Neurodivergent Talent, Dark Reading

    - https://www.darkreading.com/cybersecurity-careers/8-tips-hiring-training-neurodivergent-talent

- Book: Great People Decisions: Why They Matter So Much, Why They Are So Hard, and How You Can Master Them, Claudio Fernandez Araoz

    - https://www.goodreads.com/book/show/1282289.Great_People_Decisions

- Book, Who, Geoff Smart and Randy Street

    - https://www.goodreads.com/book/show/4989687-who (Hiring strategy)

- Book: The Power of Student Agency: Looking Beyond Grit to Close the Opportunity Gap, Anindya Kundu (Author), Pedro A. Noguera

    - https://www.goodreads.com/book/show/50670579-the-power-of-student-agency

- CSO, Women in Cyber Day finds those it celebrates 'leaving in droves'

    - https://www.csoonline.com/article/3499360/women-in-cyber-day-finds-those-it-celebrates-leaving-in-droves.html/amp/

Plan of Action for Business Leaders

- MyCyberExec

    - `https://www.mycyberexec.com/`

- Book: The 6 Types of Working Genius, Patrick Lencioni

    - `https://www.amazon.com/gp/aw/d/1637743297/ref=sspa_mw_detail_3?ie=UTF8&psc=1&sp_csd=d 2lkZ2V0TmFtZT1zcF9waG9uZV9kZXRhaWwp13NParams`

    - 6 Types Of Working Genius: Discover Your Gifts and Transform Your Work: `https://www. workinggenius.com/`

- DiSC

    - `https://www.discprofile.com/what-is-disc`

- Book: Great People Decisions: Why They Matter So Much, Why They Are So Hard, and How You Can Master Them, Claudio Fernandez Araoz

    - `https://www.goodreads.com/book/show/1282289. Great_People_Decisions`

- Varonis, Ransomware Statistics, Data, Trends, and Facts

    - `https://www.varonis.com/blog/ransomware-statistics#cost`

- Book: Sandworm, Andy Greenberg

    - `https://www.goodreads.com/en/book/show/ 41436213-sandworm`

- The Untold Story of NotPetya, the Most Devastating Cyberattack in History

  - https://www.wired.com/story/notpetya-cyberattack-ukraine-russia-code-crashed-the-world/

- How to handle today's high CISO turnover

  - https://chiefexecutive.net/how-to-handle-todays-high-ciso-turnover/

- Trellix Finds Nearly Half of CISOs to Exit the Role Without Industry Action

  - https://www.trellix.com/news/press-releases/trellix-finds-nearly-half-of-cisos-to-exit-the-role-without-industry-action/

- SEC: Cybersecurity

  - https://www.sec.gov/securities-topics/cybersecurity

- Former Chief Security Officer Of Uber Sentenced To Three Years' Probation For Covering Up Data Breach Involving Millions Of Uber User Records

  - https://www.justice.gov/usao-ndca/pr/former-chief-security-officer-uber-sentenced-three-years-probation-covering-data

- SEC Charges SolarWinds and Chief Information Security Officer with Fraud, Internal Control Failures

  - https://www.sec.gov/newsroom/press-releases/2023-227

- NIST AI Risk Management Framework

    - `https://www.nist.gov/itl/ai-risk-management-framework`

- NIST Privacy Framework

    - `https://nvlpubs.nist.gov/nistpubs/CSWP/NIST.CSWP.01162020.pdf`

- NIST Cybersecurity Framework

    - `https://www.nist.gov/quick-start-guides`

    - `https://nvlpubs.nist.gov/nistpubs/CSWP/NIST.CSWP.29.pdf`

    - `https://nvlpubs.nist.gov/nistpubs/SpecialPublications/NIST.SP.1301.pdf`

- DVMS Institute, NIST CSF Training for Business Leaders

    - `https://dvmsinstitute.com/`

- NIST Risk Management Framework

    - `https://csrc.nist.gov/projects/risk-management/about-rmf`

- FAIR Risk Management

    - `https://www.fairinstitute.org/fair-risk-management`

- ISACA, Risk Tolerance vs Risk Appetite

    - `https://www.isaca.org/resources/news-and-trends/isaca-now-blog/2022/risk-appetite-vs-risk-tolerance-what-is-the-difference`

- CIS, Reasonable Cybersecurity Guide

  - `https://www.cisecurity.org/insights/white-papers/reasonable-cybersecurity-guide`

- CISO Board Presentation Mistakes

  - `https://www.balbix.com/blog/ciso-board-presentation-mistakes/`

- Book: The Five Dysfunctions of a Team, Patrick Lencioni

  - `https://www.goodreads.com/book/show/21343.The_Five_Dysfunctions_of_a_Team`

- Ted Lasso: Believe! (part 2)

  - `https://youtu.be/JsH7yHNC-bA?si=YIA5VTUqP8gJEpzb`

- Memes

  - `https://www.balbix.com/blog/top-10-cybersecurity-memes/`

Printed in the United States
by Baker & Taylor Publisher Services